Small Miracles

WOODY VANKIRK

ISBN 978-1-64114-468-1 (paperback)
ISBN 978-1-64114-469-8 (digital)

Copyright © 2018 by Woody VanKirk

All rights reserved. No part of this publication may be reproduced, distributed, or transmitted in any form or by any means, including photocopying, recording, or other electronic or mechanical methods without the prior written permission of the publisher. For permission requests, solicit the publisher via the address below.

Christian Faith Publishing, Inc.
832 Park Avenue
Meadville, PA 16335
www.christianfaithpublishing.com

Printed in the United States of America

Dedication

Dr. Scott A. Jackson, DVM
for doing God's work here

Susan Kortyna
for doing God's work there

Contents

1. Dedication 3
2. Preface 7
3. Introduction 11
4. Me 13
5. My Cats - Kitty 20
6. My Cats - Oscar 30
7. My Cats - Honey Bunny 38
8. My Cats - Honey Honey 51
9. My Cats - Pierre 56
10. My Cats - Scaredy 62
11. Pierre & Scaredy's Not so Excellent Adventure 68
12. My Cats - Sweetie 73
13. Other cats no longer in my life but always in my heart 75
14. Other Cats no longer in My Life - Angel 80
15. Other Cats no longer in My Life - Schiz 85
16. Small Miracles 91
17. You Decide 110
18. Extra - You've Lost Your Cat - Now What? 111

Preface

If you survived an airplane crash, would you call it a miracle? If a loved one was brought back from the brink of death by the wonders of medicine, would you call it a miracle? If you saw your dog get run over by an SUV then jump up and run to you with no injuries, you would probably call that a miracle.

When we check our trusty online reference dictionary, we see that one of the definitions of miracle is:

> an effect or extraordinary event in the physical world that surpasses all known human or natural powers and is ascribed to a supernatural cause.

Even today, most people from most religious affiliations would ascribe any event as described above as being "supernatural" with most of those people attributing the miracle to God or a deity of their belief.

But what if you fell down the stairs and your only injury was a bruise? What if you dropped your keys before stepping off the curb and when you bent to pick them up, a cement truck roared past right were you would have been in the street? What if you had been thinking for some time about an old love from years gone by and then you bumped into him/her by the tire rack at Walmart?

Are those miracles? Most would say they were just a coincidence or luck. But, no, not a miracle.

If you believe in miracles for great big life-changing events in life, why can't little day-to-day events also be miracles? *Small miracles*.

This is about seven cats. This is about now, today, and my experiences with seven cats that are in my life as of this writing. This is about how these cats have helped me to renew and reinforce my belief in God and return to my Christian faith. This is about how these cats have helped me on that road and along the way to become a better person with a whole new outlook on life. One that has brought me peace that I wish I had found years ago.

This peace didn't just come to me one day out of the blue; rather it was a seed which slowly took root and grew into a belief. What happened was that I came to realize over time that many extra special events had occurred involving my cats. The more I reflected on these events, the more I became convinced that these events couldn't be mere coincidences.

I relate these experiences so that others who read about what I experienced will ask as I did if it was all just coincidence. Were these experiences all just really a run of good luck at just the right time?

I came to see that my experiences were way beyond coincidence. The odds were just too far out. If I had that kind of luck with the lottery, I'd be a billionaire. I began to see something beyond coincidence. I was seeing something supernatural. I came to see the hand of God in these events. Not coincidence, not chance, and not potluck. Not any kind of luck. I saw events being manipulated by a power way beyond coincidence.

I wish that these events, which I experienced with my cats, might help another to gain or maintain their own path to God and to their salvation. I wish you, too, to see the hand of God here.

How did it all start? How did I begin to think that I was benefiting from more than luck?

Two of my cats went missing late in December just before the Christmas holiday. Soon after they disappeared, the temperature went down to around zero for weeks before, during, and after the holidays. I thought my cats were goners.

Then on the thirty-first day of their absence, I got a phone call from a lady saying my cats were in her garage.

A few days after getting them home and thinking back about what they experienced for thirty-one days—freezing weather, no food, no water, and no heat—I began entertaining the concept of a miracle. In fact, in an interview with the local *News Sun* newspaper afterward, I actually stated that their survival was a miracle. Thirty-two days in subfreezing weather with no food or water and they were still alive.

Weeks afterward, I began thinking about some other peculiar events involving my other cats. I recalled peculiar things about these events. I saw patterns in them that I now attribute to miracles. *Small miracles.*

Life-changing and earth-shattering miracles like surviving a train wreck. No, just some teeny-tiny events with cats that I relate here. They were life changing for me.

Introduction

I wondered about those who didn't believe in God, a supreme being, the Great Spirit, or life after death. The atheists. The hard core atheists. Why didn't they believe and what would it take to make them believers?

I had experienced several events involving my cats that I believed were miraculous. I wanted to get them committed to paper with the idea of maybe getting them into print and out into the world someday. Along with that I believed that, if presented rationally, I could possibly move a few intellectually honest atheists off of their belief in nothingness and into considering the existence of a supreme being, and into believing in God.

So I wrote and printed a book. This is an expansion of that work which I had titled *Me, My Cats, and God*. I self-published it and handed out copies to my friends and that was it.

Me, My Cats, and God was something I had been composing in my mind for about four years and I finally felt compelled to get it on paper before something happened to me. As such, *Me, My Cats, and God* was a rush job.

The first thing I realized was that the title was all wrong. My cats and I are not the point of the work. The subject of the book is the miracles that occurred and their effect on me. Miracles from God. So the purpose of the rewrite was to build on that concept and expand it in the sections where it would be helpful and add to the narrative.

The chapters about the cats have been enhanced with additional narrative. They are about specific incidents that I have come to identify as *small miracles*.

There is some bio about each cat to allow the reader to get a feel for each feline personality, but there are no cat and butterfly anecdotes, no ball of yarn events, and no feline cuteness typically found in books about cats. In this book, the cats are the supporting cast for the main event, the *small miracles*.

And, yes, there are religious overtones as well, but only as I have come to understand it. There is no preaching, just commentary. The commentary herein was inspired by the *small miracles* I write about. I write how they inspired me. There is some religious viewpoints from my perspective in section 17, so if you absolutely can't take it, then just bypass that section.

Those religious parts are from me. They are from the heart and from my limited knowledge of the Bible. So if I have stepped on anyone's religious toes, it is all me and it was not done to start any theological back and forth.

All cat persons will enjoy this.

If you are an atheist or an atheist cat person, you will enjoy reading about my cats. This is not fire and brimstone rammed down your throat. This is only about seven cats and their lives with me. As an atheist, how could the events of seven cats change your religious convictions? Go ahead take the plunge. You can form your own conclusions afterward.

If you are an agnostic cat person, you will enjoy reading about my cats. You will be faced with two choices and I hope you see the miracles I saw.

If you are a nonpracticing believer cat person, I urge you to read this book. It may stoke up those embers and get the flames going again. All nonpracticing believers who like cats will enjoy reading about these cats.

If you are just a run-of-the-mill animal lover, I'm sure you will appreciate this book if just for the cat parts.

Me

I would rather not write about myself and not include this part and just get on to the cats and their miracles. However, for you to understand how these miracles affected my life, I have to tell you about my life.

I was raised a Christian, going to church on Sunday and to Sunday school and church events while growing up. My family went to whatever church my parents felt comfortable with without regard to its tenants or denomination. We didn't go to a Catholic church as I was told that we were "Protestant."

Around the age of fourteen, I began going to an evangelical church with a friend. His mother took us. I really got into the various activities, and as long as he and his mom were going, I got a ride with them.

My parents were not very enthused about my newfound activities. Though they were not interested in my new church or its activities, they did not discourage me either. This was about the same time as they stopped going to church. Still, I continued with my new church, going to as many activities as I could as long as I could get a ride there. It was while going to this church that I accepted Jesus Christ as my Lord and Savior.

As I learned more about the Bible, and about faith I began to have questions. Many questions. And confusion. Much confusion. I got my ride there and back and that was it. I had no one to talk to about what I was learning and no one to ask about all the questions I had. I found myself working out the answers to my questions on my own. I probably came up with a few incorrect conclusions here and there.

By the age of sixteen my religious questions and confusion were put to the ultimate test by girls, puberty, girls, my social life, girls, cars, and girls. Add to that the angst of getting through a high school that I had complete disdain for. Moreover, at this time, my family began to unravel. Looking back, there's no doubt this disintegration started long before but this is the point where I realized something was going on with my parents' relationship.

This was when I put God on the backburner of my life. I was seventeen and looking at the prospect of my local draft board reaching out to me with a friendly invitation. It was difficult for me to focus on God and matters of faith with so many distractions and facing the breakup of my family.

That sounds like an excuse. Looking back even now, it even seems like an excuse. And a lame one. I can't remember my exact mindset then, and I wonder if there were some other issues involved. I was being tested and I failed.

In any case, there was no one to talk to about these concerns. No one was there to motivate me, and I lacked the self-motivation to persevere in my faith.

By the time I graduated from high school, my parents were separated and divorce soon followed. I ended up with my father, while my brother and sister ended up in another city staying with my mother.

At that time, I was all alone. Even though I shared an apartment with my dad, I was still alone. We did not do much together. In fact, we did nothing together. My dad took up drinking again after his seventeen-year abstinence, and I had no wish to join him.

I was alone without family and friends. I was also without church, church sermons, church preachers, church do-gooders, and the confusion I got from going to church.

At least that's the way it seemed at the time. When I was going to church with my friend and his mother, I had been saved and had given myself to Jesus Christ. Yet here I was thinking I was all alone. I was not alone but I was too dumb to realize it. God had not abandoned me—I had abandoned Him.

God does not abandon man. Man abandons God. I am proof of that.

From the time I graduated from high school, I had attempted to join the US Army three times. My first time saw me driving to an army base in New York to sign up. On the way there, the tread on my cheap retread tire on my cheap car came partially loose. Before I could pull over and stop, it had whipped around in the rear wheel well and knocked the gas tank loose. I was left next to the highway with my gas tank hanging out and gas leaking all over. That ended my first attempt to enlist.

My second attempt to join the army happened when a guy I worked with in the factory wanted to join up and disappear as he had just found out his girlfriend was pregnant. He said he was going over right after work to join the army, so I told him I would go with him. What the heck?

Upon arrival at the recruiter, we discovered the office was closed. I can't remember why, but it was closed with a handwritten notice explaining why and when it would reopen.

My third time trying to join the army was a week after the second attempt mentioned above. This time, I was going alone, as my coworker had reevaluated his desire to join up. This was in early 1965. Vietnam had that effect on a lot of men back then.

As I approached the door of the recruiting office, it opened, and two huge sergeants emerged carrying briefcases. When they saw me, they asked what I was there for, and I told them I wanted to sign up. They told me something about an appointment they were on their way to and I had to come back tomorrow. So much for joining the army.

So in the aftermath of my family's breakup and a pending draft notice, I went and joined the navy.

No problems there, and soon—very soon—I was off to exotic locales with Uncle Sam as my travel agent.

In the military, I had control over my life within military guidelines, and I chose not to go to church. It was my decision, not that of the military. In fact, the military went out of their way to make places of worship available to those who wished to practice their faith. I passed, and on official military forms I often entered "agnostic" in the spaces to indicate my religion. Agnostic, not atheist. I was so very modern.

However, I must not have been too agnostic as I have the letter "P" for Protestant on my dog tags, and by the time I left the military, I had stopped referring to myself as agnostic.

After the military, I was never antireligion, but I was never very proreligion either. I did not ridicule anyone for their religious beliefs no matter what their beliefs were. Even when there were times when other people's religious beliefs really irked me, like Witnesses knocking on my door at 8:00 AM.

Although I got out of the military during the time of peace and love, making a living and paying my bills was mostly in the forefront of my life, and I found I was usually too financially disadvantaged for any peace and love.

One smart thing I did after getting a place to live was to get myself a couple of cats. Now I had making a living, paying bills, and caring for my cats on the front burner of my life. Guess who was still on the back burner? More lame excuses.

By the mid '70s, I knew I believed in God. I knew I had never stopped believing. Strangely, my cats caused the reemergence of my belief, and that started me back on track to faith.

It started one day in my backyard with my two cats. One of them was basking in the sun, not aware of my presence. He was beneath a bush, yet some sunbeams were right on him. He wasn't asleep, just sitting with his head up and his eyes almost but not quite closed and he was just enjoying the moment. He was comfy with the sun beaming on him; he was safe and not hungry. Birds were chirping and the bugs weren't bothering him. He was at peace with himself and with his world.

This fascinated me, and I watched him for about fifteen minutes, trying to imagine what was going on in his mind, in his cat world. It was during this observation that I realized I was seeing something special. No, not a cat enjoying the sun, I was seeing something more, something special. This cat was doing something more than just basking, but I didn't know what.

I was thinking of my cats, then all cats and their special ties to humanity over the centuries. I gave this much thought and considered the presence of cats in human life and now in my life. Somewhere in all my thinking and pondering, I got around to God.

I knew, absolutely knew, that my cat could not be the result of some primordial piece of protoplasmic slime getting hit with lightning seven or eight billion years ago. I could not believe that my cat basking in the sun had evolved from some Jurassic reptile seventy million years ago. I couldn't believe that my cat was a random occurrence that happened under the all-inclusive explanation of *evolution*.

The sun that warmed my cat that summer day was just right, not too close to the earth and not too far away. Gravity was just right and so was the air we were breathing. I could not then and do not now believe that all this was the result of ages and ages of cosmic goop mixing, and by pure luck becoming the earth that my cat and I were on. This could not be the evolution that many scientists believe and would have us believe, and this definitely could not be coincidence. This had to be more. This was the beginning of my road back to God and to faith.

Don't jump to conclusions. Despite my revelation then, I did not go to any extremes. I did not begin attending church nor did you see me by the interstate exit holding up a *John 3:16* sign.

Living through the '70s and then through the '80s and the '90s and during all my trips up and down on the ladder of success, I saw religious hypocrisy running rampant throughout the business world that was my life then. Business deals being done in the name of God, business deals being done for the benefit of God, and shady dealings done by men who claimed to be men of God.

Yet all the time, their business was for man, the deals were for man, and the rewards were for man. Nothing was about God, nothing was for God, and nothing was for the glory of God.

During that time, I considered myself a pretty astute businessman. I was always very gung-ho when it came to anything that would benefit my company and very suspicious of anything that could hurt it. In reflection, I must honestly say that some of my business dealings were illegal, immoral, and unethical, along with those that could easily pass as "un-Christian."

At the pinnacle of all my successes, I was a person full of pride for myself and arrogant toward others. I was full of myself over the heights to which I had ascended and for what I had accomplished. I had achieved some pretty lofty heights, and I had done it without the benefit of a college degree. Such were the opportunities in my field in those days.

With all the success, I still kept God on that back burner. I forged onward, ever onward, forgetting that *pride goeth before the fall* (Proverbs 16:18).

And the fall did come. And it was big. The climb back up was painful, economically difficult, and slow. I never did rise back up to my former lofty heights.

That brings this narrative up to the present, and to the place where I began seeing miracles with this bunch of cats I have.

When the events with these seven cats were occurring, I began to see a few too many coincidences and way too much luck. Coincidence and luck didn't fully explain the results I was seeing. I began to see divine involvement, divine intervention, the hand of God. I hope you will agree with my conclusions.

I would like you to believe that these were indeed miracles that were bestowed upon my cats. I would like you to believe in a higher power. I would like you to believe in a higher authority. I would like you to believe in Almighty God.

If you can believe that the *small miracles* I write about here can happen at such a small level to something so insignificant in the universe as a cat, then perhaps you can come to believe in miracles at a higher level, believe in all of God's great miracles for all of mankind, and believe in God and His love.

Beyond that, there's very much material available that can guide you further. But first, you must *believe*.

Everybody believes in something. In the US today, most people profess to be Christians. Other religions are making headway as the gates to immigration are opened wider and the standards for entry get lower. As such, the Christian population will continue to be diluted with other beliefs, cults, and religions.

Atheists claim to believe in nothing, especially not in God or in any god. Yet they have a belief. It is the belief of atheism. Atheist groups are active in their beliefs, demanding the removal of religious symbols, mostly Christian, every day from public venues on the grounds that the symbols are offensive. How can something that they don't believe in be offensive?

In any newspaper, any magazine, any internet article, or on any media broadcast, you see how hard the atheists fight for their belief system. In the courts, they fight legal battles to ban religion and any religious trappings from their everyday life. You don't fight that hard or spend that kind of money for something you don't believe in. If you dig deep enough with an atheist, you typically find that behind their altar of atheism is their real god—they believe in the government.

If you are a nonbeliever, read what I have written and see if these words nudge you just a bit closer to my belief. See if these words can't get your brain cells agitated enough to see if you can reconsider your views on nonbelief.

But enough about me. This is about seven cats and some *small miracles* involving them that made a profound impact on my life and my relationship with God.

I will be telling you about Kitty, Oscar, Honey Bunny, Honey Honey, Pierre, Scaredy, and Sweetie.

You will meet them each in a section just for them. In these sections, I will relate some of their characteristics and some special events with these cats. I will not highlight the *small miracles* so see if you can recognize them as you read. Do not worry if you fail to see the *small miracle* with these events. The miracles will be covered in a later section.

My Cats - Kitty

Kitty is my senior citizen. I have had her since September 1999. It would be more correct to say that she had me since September 1999. I suspect she was born about May or June that year. As this goes to press, she is seventeen and a half.

The way Kitty and I came together is quite extraordinary.

I was at my job one day. A job in which I had turned in my two-week notice and still had one more week to work. I was working on the roof on the tenth floor, looking for a water leak that was getting into the space below. It was a flat roof and there was no telling just where the leak was.

There was a water outlet on the roof and the plan was to run water over sections of the roof and monitor below to see where the leak was coming from. The hose I needed to do this was on the ground attached to the lawn sprinkler.

I went down ten floors and outside to get the hose. I unhooked it from the faucet and the sprinkler, rolled it up, and prepared to haul it up to the roof. Doing this put me in this location for about five minutes.

Just as I was ready to hoist the hose and go back to the roof, I heard a meow. I looked around. Nothing. Another meow. I still saw nothing, but I knew I had heard a meow.

Then, from beneath a bush almost at my feet emerged a tiny black kitten. It looked up at me with trepidation and let out another meow. I squatted down and held out my hand to it. Instead of coming to me, it ran back under the bush! I assumed I scared it and I was going to go back to the roof and get going on the job before someone noticed that I was not there.

But from beneath the bush, the kitten emerged once again; but this time, another kitten followed it! It was a nifty chocolate brown color, and this time, they both came up to me and I was able to pet them.

Long story short, I ended up with the black kitten and my coworker took the brown one. I brought her home that day.

My intention was to find a home for her, and because of this, I never gave her a name. I just referred to her as "Kitty" while I looked around for someone who wanted a kitten.

During this time, one of my other cats, Microcat (Mike), started going downhill, and within weeks, I knew he wouldn't be with me much longer. So being the proactive far-thinking person I am, I decided to keep Kitty. This way, my second cat, Schiz, wouldn't be alone. I have always believed that house cats need at least one other cat with them, so I have always had two cats.

For a short while, I had three cats until Microcat passed, and then it was just two cats, Kitty and Schiz (pronounced as "skits").

Kitty played a part in my struggle to get back on the path to salvation in regards to prayer. Here's how she came to play her part in my journey.

I had recently said a prayer. Yes, "a" prayer. To set the stage, at my job at that time, a coworker, Joe, had come in one day and was enlisting all employees to say a prayer for "Poppi." It seems Poppi, his father-in-law, was not doing so well, health wise. Things weren't looking good. I can attest to this as I had seen Poppi at a cookout at Joe's a few weeks previously. To me, Poppi looked like one of those men you see in those World War II clips of the liberation of the concentration camps.

Joe must have asked everyone at least three times that day to not to forget to say a prayer for Poppi. That night, I said a prayer for Poppi. That prayer was my first prayer in probably thirty-five years.

Poppi got better.

Now on to Kitty and the part she played in prayer in my life. This was at the time when I had six cats.

One day, I got home from work and discovered that a cat had used the rear corner of the living room as their potty place. I found the same thing the next day and again on the day after that.

I was really getting quite disturbed as cat urine does nasty things to hardwood floors. I needed to find out which one was the guilty feline, so one at a time I picked each one up and carried them to where the "evidence" was in the corner. Of all the cats, Kitty was the only one that squirmed and tried to jump out of my arms when presented with the evidence. I knew I had the culprit.

I tried the usual admonitions like putting her nose in it while scolding her. As the days went by, the results were the same—a mess in the corner. It got so bad that Kitty would hide when I got home because she knew I was going to take her over to the mess and yell at her. I had also escalated to smacking her rump with a rolled up newspaper.

MY CATS - KITTY

At this time, the cat litter box was in the basement. I had always kept it in the basement since day one cat one. It was in by the sink and furnace, and Kitty had been and still was using it. I know because I was monitoring her.

From what I could tell, she would only go in the living room about once a day. Why was the mystery, and it was a challenge for me to figure out what was going on.

Meanwhile, nothing changed as the days went by, and my patience was growing short. Kitty was still using the corner as a potty, and I was at my wits end as to what to do. Things almost got out of hand when I got so mad and I almost hurt Kitty. I hate to admit this, but I am also glad that I caught myself before I did any harm to her.

The situation was now so bad Kitty was now terrified if I just picked her up for any reason. She automatically assumed I was going to take her in the living room, swat her with the newspaper, and yell at her.

I decided to try prayer and began praying daily for an end to this. Keep in mind this would now be my second prayer in about thirty-five years. What I was praying for was for God to send an angel to speak to Kitty and tell her not to keep using the living room as her cat box.

In the meantime, I stopped taking Kitty into the living room and swatting her and yelling at her. I knew she knew she was doing wrong; I just needed to find out why. Further chastisement of Kitty would serve no further purpose. I just cleaned up the mess and prayed daily for God to send that angel, and the sooner the better.

One day, God answered my prayers. No, He didn't send an angel to tell Kitty to stop making messes in the living room. That would have been too easy, and God does not always make things that easy for us. If we need something very much He will show us how to obtain it. Sometimes, we may have to work for it, and that was exactly how He answered my prayer.

The mystery was solved one day while I was in the basement. I was sitting such that I had a view of the steps coming down in to the basement.

At that time, a coffee table was situated in a direct visual line with the stair steps. There was a blanket spread across it, and my two new cats, Honey Bunny and Honey Honey, loved to sit there together. More about these cats later.

On this occasion, I was sitting on the coffee table with Honey Bunny and Honey Honey. Kitty was at the top of the steps, peering downward. She would come down a step, stop, and watch. Then she would come down another step, stop, and watch. Again, she came down another step and watched.

As I was watching, I wondered what the heck was she watching. I observed all this from where I was sitting.

At the same time this was happening, I noticed Honey Honey keeping a keen eye on Kitty. Hmmm. This went on until Kitty got about two steps from the bottom. At this point, Honey Honey came flying off the coffee table, ran across to the steps, ran up to Kitty, and swatted her a good one.

Kitty went fleeing back up the steps.

My eyes were opened! I saw the light! It wasn't a burning bush or a pillar of fire, but suddenly, I knew. It was so obvious. Kitty was coming to use the litter box in the basement, but if she came down when Honey Honey was on guard on the coffee table, Honey Honey would chase her back up the steps. Mystery solved!

I installed a second cat box in the back bedroom. No more messes in the living room. Prayers answered! Kitty now had an alternate place to do her business if Honey Honey was standing guard in the basement.

My prayers had been answered and Kitty has never used the living room corner again. Except I now had two boxes to maintain, along with all the dust and tracked litter to deal with. Oh, joy. I put up with this for years and things changed.

I had changes around the basement and I had more cats. Kitty was now able to walk past Honey Honey without getting terrorized as Honey Honey had matured years ago and stopped her silly game of keeping Kitty from coming down to the basement. So I reverted once again to one litter box in the basement.

But I had another litter box incident. I started finding pee on the kitchen floor. (Thanks to myself for getting new vinyl put down just a few years before.) This incident didn't go on as long as the previous, and I soon discovered it was Kitty again. And the cause was the same as before!

Only this time it wasn't Honey Honey doing it. It was a new cat, Sweetie, and she was doing the same thing Honey Honey had done years before. Sweetie would be hanging out in the kitchen, and when Kitty would try to pass through to go down the stairs, Sweetie would charge her and send her packing back into the rest of the house. Kitty, not being able to get past the kitchen, took to going on the kitchen floor.

I reinstalled the second litter box in the back bedroom and no more problems from then to now.

Kitty is still with me and seems to be in good health. She has lost three of her canine teeth and is showing obvious signs of aging. Her black hair is becoming rust colored, along with some areas getting gray, and she is a little slower.

Kitty was quite antisocial toward the other cats and would be very content to be the only cat in this house. She resists the efforts of the other cats to be friends and she remains a loner. She does seem to be devoted to being around me. She craves affection, and at times, I can't even walk past her without her reaching out and hooking me with a claw. I do my best to accommodate her. I reluctantly admit that I spoil her.

She is a good lap cat and sleeps in the bed with me. Kitty does not care for Oscar, and will hiss or swipe at him if he gets too close. And she really, really doesn't care for Honey Bunny. She will hiss and spit at Honey Bunny and leave the room if Honey Bunny is around.

Years ago, when I was getting ready for work, I noticed Kitty was something of a "pirate." When all the other cats would gather around in the morning at feeding time, anxiously awaiting their food, Kitty would bypass all that and jump from the table onto the counter where I was preparing their food. There, she would stick her head in the bowl and start eating before I was even done emptying the food can, and thus, beating her roommates to the chow. I called this a "pirate raid."

As Kitty advanced in age, I became concerned about her leaps back and forth from counter to table. I have since taken to putting a small dab of food in a dish and putting it on the table just for Kitty. This has become a tradition, and I don't worry about Kitty leaping tall counters at a single bound.

When I first brought Kitty home as a kitten, she loved to insinuate herself in the crook of my left arm and snooze. She would do this no matter what I was doing, but mostly when I was on the computer. It didn't matter. As a kitten, I was able to hold her there for up to an hour with no problem as she was so small.

Then she grew up. Recently, it seems she has been trying to relive those moments. At least that's what I call it. She gets in the crook of my arm like she did then. The only thing is she doesn't fit. But she insists. So with her head on my shoulder, her paws in my armpit, and her back end on my right shoulder, she takes up position and tries to nap. Unfortunately, I can't maintain her full-grown weight, and she never gets to stay there very long before I have to change position and adjust her and my arm.

But she keeps trying.

As of this writing, Kitty is older and she no longer beats up Oscar. She just takes the occasional swipe at him. She still would be perfectly happy if all the other cats got beamed into the cornfield.

I remember that day when Kitty first came to me. Out she came from under that bush she was hiding beneath and looked up at me with that look. The look she gave me that day I keep alive and well in memory. The memory of how she stood by my feet with her face turned up to me. I cherished that memory.

While writing this, I realized I still get that look. I get it every day, many times. None of the other cats look up at me like that. I will hear her special meow and look down and there she is, looking up at me. The same look on her face and the same angle to her neck as on that day back then. But I had never realized it.

I have been letting Kitty outside but only when I can be there to watch her. I think Kitty appreciates this as she has spent years looking out the back door, and now she gets to see it for herself. There is catnip planted in the yard and Kitty discovered it her second day out. She loves it. Plus, she gets to go in the garage and sneak some of Scaredy's dry cat food. Scaredy was at first intimidated by Kitty. Maybe it was her color; but they have met and touched noses and that seems to be that.

And Kitty got to chase birds and squirrels. She's no spring chicken and she doesn't stand a chance to catch anything, and I think she knows it, but it's good to see her getting about like that.

Kitty's age doesn't seem to slow her down and I must watch her like a hawk. She loves to go exploring, and I constantly have to go next door and chase her back into her yard.

One day, I couldn't find her for about ten minutes anywhere, even next door. I was getting close to panic when Kitty suddenly came running flat out from around the neighbor's house and across the back of the house coming toward her yard. Right behind her was Zach, the boy from next door to me on the other side. He had been walking home from his friend's house and spotted Kitty about five houses down from me, exploring bushes.

Zach recognized her and planned to pick her up and bring her back home. Kitty wasn't having any of that, thus accounting for her sprint back to her own yard.

Some years back, Kitty began sneezing. Some allergy or something, I don't know what. She would blast off about five or six sneezes in a row and then she was good for a while. And she would do that a few times a day each and every day.

One day, she started sneezing and didn't stop. After some hours of this, I scooped her up and took her to see Dr. Jackson. He gave her something to stop the sneezing and she is back to sneezing five or six times in a row multiple times a day.

Meanwhile, Kitty has taken to pawing me when she wants attention, usually for food. For an old cat, I take this as a good sign as she has a good appetite. Anyway, she will paw my face when she wants to get my attention. It is a very gently nudge, just placing her paw on my cheek. She will do this when I am reading sometimes, but mostly she does this when I'm asleep.

What's the problem? The problem is that Kitty, like all the cats, has her claws and they are sharp. And they extend past the fur on Kitty's paws. Which means when she gives me that oh-so-gentle nudge with her paw while I'm asleep, I am getting an oh-so-gentle nudge from four very sharp needles.

Needless to say, I wake up faster than I ever could with any alarm clock. And Kitty, well, her mission was accomplished as I then attend to whatever it was she wanted from me.

There is one more incident involving Kitty that you will read about in the "Other Cats No Longer in My Life but Always in My Heart" section.

My Cats - Oscar

In 2003, while at another of my many jobs, a kitten wandered into our shop. It was summer and the bay doors were always open. This kitten wouldn't leave day after day, even though the big doors were always open. After a few days, the poor thing began wailing. We all knew it was hungry, but it was well hidden behind a bunch of steel and wouldn't come out to us. We left it alone, figuring it would come out when it got hungry enough. It didn't.

The second weekend was approaching where this kitten would have been in the shop with nothing to eat that we knew of. It did have toilets to drink from. Jimmy, who ran the shop, got a trap from Orkin, which had an office a few doors up from us. His intention was to trap the cat and take it to the pound.

I went home at lunch and brought back cat food to lure it into the trap. When I left work that Friday, I realized that on the off chance the kitten went for the bait at 6:00 PM that Friday, it would be stuck in the trap until someone came in on Monday. I didn't like the thought of a cat trapped in a cage for two days, so at 9:00 PM, I went over and checked the trap. No cat. The same when I checked at 7:00 AM and 1:00 PM on Saturday.

When I checked at 5:00 PM that Saturday, there it was, a little black kitten inside the trap with a clean-as-a-whistle empty cat food can. However, not having planned beyond this point as what to do after I caught it, I took it home.

At home, I let him loose as I do with any new cat. He was scared of all the other cats, let out a wail, and ran off and hid. He was scared of the other cats and was scared of me. It took over a month to assure him that I was not a threat to him. During this time, I kept him alone in the back bedroom. After about six weeks, he finally had enough nerve to venture out into the house.

It didn't take long to realize that Kitty did not like Oscar. In fact, she was downright hostile to him. I figured that must be the reason why Oscar was always hiding in the basement, to keep out of Kitty's way. He had found a hidey-hole inside and beneath some cabinets, just small enough for a kitten, and Kitty couldn't get to him there. I would have to coax him out to feed him and he was always on the lookout for Kitty. So I became very protective to him.

One time, to protect him from that bad old Kitty, I held him on my chest while lying on the couch. Kitty came looking for him, and when she saw where he was, she sat down about four feet away from us, glaring at him. He was skittish at her presence, but I had him on my chest and I kept calming him and telling him not to worry and that I would protect him.

Kitty, however, didn't care what I had to say. From her perch four feet away, she ran up my legs, swiped him, and took off running. This happened so fast I didn't even react until it was over. Oscar, meanwhile, took off to his hidey-hole.

Sometimes, he would get caught out in the open and couldn't get past Kitty to get to his hiding nook. I soon discovered that Oscar had developed a unique way of keeping Kitty away from him—he would poop and then roll around in it. It worked, and Kitty stayed away from him. Guess who got to clean Oscar afterward? Luckily for me Oscar stopped doing this after some weeks.

Oscar grew up and can kick Kitty's butt now but he doesn't know it, so he is still leery of her, and Kitty still swipes at him whenever she has the chance. However, at Kitty's age, her swipes are more of just a waving of a paw in his general direction.

At this point in the timeline, I had three cats—Schiz, Kitty, and Oscar.

Oscar personally caused me to have to redo my living room, hallway, and some parts of my upstairs bedrooms. Here's what this little bundle of sweetness did.

Years before I had finished my living room and hallway with wallpaper. I had picked out a pattern that I felt I would not get bored with and would not become dated or look old fashioned as time went by. I was successful and thought I would never have to redo those areas again. Ever.

Until one day when I noticed a curved tear in the hallway wallpaper. The tear was about thirty inches up from the floor, about eight inches in length, and circular in shape. I had no idea what caused it, but I was able to repair it using wallpaper repair glue. I suspected a cat.

What a great detective I am using deductive reasoning. But who or what else is in the house to have done it? I couldn't connect the curved tear with anything a cat would do, so I remained bewildered.

Over the next few months, these wallpaper tears began to appear in the living room and the two upstairs bedrooms, as well as additional tears in the hallway. There was even one attempted tear on the kitchen wallpaper, but the kitchen wallpaper is vinyl and much tougher.

After some time, the tears became bigger and were becoming too severe to repair. One big tear in the living room I was able to hide by strategically relocating a chair in front of it. In the upstairs bedrooms, I was able to cover the damage with some sections of paneling that matched the décor and looked like they belonged.

This had been going on over a period of about a year and a half, and I was going bananas trying to figure where these tears were from. But the tears were getting bigger and higher up, and finally I could no longer hide or repair all of them.

I then began a two-and-a-half-year project to strip all the wallpaper from the living room and hallway and redo the walls with paint.

This two-and-a-half-year period was due to my attitude then. I just couldn't get motivated. I liked the wallpaper and that's why I put it up in the first place. Now, here I was stripping it off and prepping the walls to accept paint. So what should have only taken a few weeks of motivated labor took me two and a half years of foot dragging and feeling sorry for myself for having to do this job.

Fortunately, further circular wallpaper tears did not appear in the other rooms, which still had wallpaper on their walls.

Sometime after all this two-and-a-half-year paper stripping and repainting was complete, I was at my computer. I just happened to turn my head at just the right time to see Oscar leap high up in the air. When he got to the top of his leap, he swiped his paw in a circular motion. I heard his claws scrape across a piece of the paneling, which I had placed to cover previous tears in the wallpaper.

Oscar was just trying to nail a bug that was fluttering around. Mystery solved! And so all those tears in the wallpaper weren't Oscar's fault at all. It was mine because some bugs got in the house.

One day, Oscar had a very close call—literally life and death. Here's what happened.

In the basement by the litter boxes, I have a cheap air filter hooked to a motion detector. It filters out some of the litter dust that gets kicked up. It comes on when the cats show up and goes off a few minutes after they leave. I put air fresheners in the filter to freshen the air in the litter box area when the filter is blowing.

One Friday afternoon I was cleaning the litter boxes. When I was done, I was going to leave, but at the last minute, don't ask me why, I decided to change the air freshener inside the filter. I didn't have to do it that day, or even the next day, but I chose to do at that time.

Halfway through the job, I looked over to see Oscar in the litter box. This was very unusual, as Oscar just does not go in the litter box if I am around. So to make him more relaxed, I left the area. A minute later, I returned and he was still in the same position in the litter box. I left again, and, again, returned in another minute. Oscar was still in position in the litter box. I left again, and this time, I waited outside the doorway. Soon, Oscar came strolling out. When I tried to pet him, he scooted past me like he does when he thinks he did something wrong.

I went to the litter box and realized that one of my worst cat fears had happened. The litter was bone dry. I knew immediately that Oscar was plugged and could not go pee. This is not a really rare happening in male cats, but it is a killer if not caught quickly. I knew I needed to get Oscar to the doctor immediately.

Oscar showed, once again, that psychic ability of cats to know when they are going to the vet and he immediately disappeared. After much tribulation and trials, I finally captured him and got him to the doctor.

At the vet Dr. Jackson was doing surgery and was unavailable to see Oscar. Luckily x-rays and Dr. Anita Kinscher confirmed that he was indeed plugged. Dr. Kinscher outlined the plan of attack to treat him.

I had to return at 6:00 PM to get Oscar and take him to the emergency animal clinic. Oscar needed thirty-six hours of care and observation, and my vet would be closing from Saturday afternoon until Monday morning, and it was Friday.

Due to the fact that I took Oscar to the doctor at the very beginning of his problem, everything went well and I was able to bring him home Saturday about 6:00 PM.

The other cats were there to welcome him home except Honey Bunny and Sweetie. Apparently, because of all the medical smells he picked up while at the doctors, these two didn't recognize him. By the next day, Honey Bunny was OK with Oscar; but weeks later, Sweetie still didn't know who he was and would fight with him and screech at him.

Oscar took to hiding out upstairs for about six months. Eventually, things cooled down and Oscar and Sweetie were back to being buddies. I sure felt sorry for him when he was on the lam from Sweetie, considering what he had gone through early on with Kitty.

Oscar still likes to stay to himself and rarely comes around for attention. After Oscar's veterinary experience, he and Sweetie slowly got to know each other for the second time, and now, they get along and play around once in a while. But it was a very slow process.

Oscar is still very shy and timid, definitely not an alpha male. He is easily spooked by a sudden move on my part. Even if I drop something, he takes off running.

He comes around about once a month for some attention, which he really likes. Otherwise, he keeps to himself and has several hidey spots where he can retreat to. Despite his desire to get some affection from me from time to time, Oscar has never ever climbed onto my lap. Not even an exploratory visit.

Oscar had never given up trying to be friends with Kitty. He head butts her and rubs against her. Kitty, being the snot she is, ignores his efforts, but he is making headway.

Oscar is crazy about cat treats and comes running at the sound of any cellophane bag being opened. Because of Oscar getting plugged, I removed all dry food from the daily diet of all the cats. This is to prevent him from plugging again. I do put out a small bowl of dry food at weeklong intervals for the cats and they all enjoy it, especially Oscar. By spacing out the dry food feedings, my theory is that anything in Oscar that would build up and plug him will get flushed out over the intervals.

There's one thing about Oscar that makes me laugh. I laugh and wonder at the same time. The cats have an electric drinking fountain water dish. One of those that recirculates and filters the water and then pours it out in a small stream.

The cats all like it just fine and drink from it when thirsty. Oscar can't seem to grasp the fundamentals of this device though, and when he wants a drink, he sticks his head right in and the water stream pours down on his head. He drinks away all the while the water stream is pouring over his head. None of the other cats had any problem getting a drink either right from the stream or from the pool in the bottom.

Go figure.

My Cats - Honey Bunny

I wanted a kitten to replace Angel. (See "Other Cats in My Life - Angel" at the end to read about Angel.)

A friend of mine, Susan Kortyna, was a cat lover and cat caregiver. She often took in strays, and at this time, she had a bunch of kittens she couldn't find a home for and was going to have to take them to the shelter. She had about eight of her own and couldn't take any more. I told her I could take a kitten.

Great, it was all set. Then Susan asked if I could possibly take two cats. The kitten I wanted plus an adult cat. She had one that she had to keep apart from her others and she was going to have to take it to the shelter. I hemmed, hawed and dragged my feet, but I finally agreed to take the second cat. It didn't take much cajoling, I admit.

Susan was very pretty and I thought I could really impress her by helping out and taking this second cat.

Over July 4, 2004, she brought my two new cats to my house. Two females. The kitten, who I later named Honey Honey, happened to be the niece of the adult. The adult I soon named Honey Bunny. At that time, I could care less about Honey Bunny, as I was all excited over my new kitten.

Honey Honey, a kitten, probably confused and scared from being uprooted from her previous existence, promptly ran and hid in the basement. In fact, she pretty much avoided me for over a year and made the basement her living space. More about her later.

Honey Bunny was different. Very different. Somehow, she knew that she was home. She knew this before I knew it. From the moment she was out of her cage, she was at peace and comfortable in her new surroundings and with the other cats, Kitty, Oscar, and Schiz. She seemed to know who I was and what I was there for and she immediately set about bonding with me. She used every opportunity to get in my face, which she would really do with head butts and nose rubbing. Literally, she would butt my face, touch her nose to my nose, and then rub against my face, my hand, arm, or leg.

Within two days, she had worked her wily charms and I had bonded strongly with her—this cat that I didn't really want, this cat I took just to make my friend Susan happy.

Honey Bunny stayed in the basement a lot. I think it was because of Honey Honey, as she kind of became a substitute mother to Honey Honey. In fact, for about six months, whenever I would see Honey Bunny, I would see Honey Honey right behind her. It was as if Honey Honey was a pull toy that Honey Bunny was pulling around. For about a year, the only time I could get near Honey Honey was at the food dish. She would follow Honey Bunny up the stairs to eat and then, and only then, would I get to pet her.

At this point, I have five cats: Schiz, Kitty, Oscar, Honey Bunny, and Honey Honey.

Honey Bunny is unique. Very unique and I have many interesting anecdotes about her.

When I got her, she was a skinny little thing with more hair than body. She was skinny but there was a reason for this. It seems Honey Bunny brought some friends with her when she moved in. Protozoans were living in her. Not good.

After two trips to Dr. Jackson and a lot of expensive tests and medicine, Honey Bunny got better. Then she got bigger! Much bigger. Her weight doubled and she grew. She changed so much that Kitty became extremely wary of her and then very intimidated by her and remains so to this day.

But the medical troubles were not yet over for Honey Bunny.

Toward the end of July 2007, I went to bed about 1:30 AM. I had just turned out the light, and as usual, I heard the scratching of Honey Bunny's claws on the floor as she was strolling into the bedroom. Each night, she would come on the bed as soon as I got in. Sometimes, she would stay the night and sometimes just five minutes. But always when I went to bed.

On this night, I heard her at the foot of the bed and anticipated her leap onto the bed. Instead, I heard an unbelievable scream. It was a scream of pain and it was followed by the sound of cat claws scrabbling away down the hall. The sound went through the kitchen and then I heard *thump, thump, thump* going down the stairs to the basement. It was Honey Bunny and something awful had happened to her! Something bad.

I ran to the basement to see what was happening. I found Honey Bunny hiding in a cupboard by Oscar's old hidey-hole. I had to coax her out. Her eyes were real big and glassy and she had a look on her face I cannot describe. I carried her to an open area and set her down.

Honey Bunny couldn't walk. All she could do was scoot along, dragging her back end around with her. She looked like a dog, scooting along the rug to scratch its butt, but this did not look funny. It was heartbreaking.

At 2:15 in the morning, I was at the animal emergency clinic. I left about 4:15 with a semidiagnosis and I was told to get her to a certain specialist vet in Akron, 40 miles away, but first I had to go through my regular vet. I had her at the vet at 7:00 AM.

After being late getting to work that day, I left at noon to return to the vet. Thanks to an understanding boss. Dr. Jackson had checked her over and looked over the tests done by the emergency clinic. He also had set me up with an immediate appointment with the specialty clinic in Akron, and by 1:15 PM, I was on my way to Akron with Honey Bunny.

I was at the clinic, really a very elaborate animal hospital, until 9:30 that night. I had to leave Honey Bunny there for the night. More tests.

I made it to work the next day and returned to Akron by 5:00 PM. There, I was told all kinds of things that weren't wrong with Honey Bunny, but I wasn't told what was wrong. A whole slew of specialists had examined her. I was told that she might have suffered a spinal stroke. What in the world was a spinal stroke? I was told there was nothing more that could be done medically for her.

They told me to take her home and confine her and not let her walk or move at all, and to bring her back in five weeks for further diagnosis.

I took Honey Bunny home to confine her like the doctors said. But just where do you confine a cat? In fact, how do you even go about confining a cat? Cats aren't noted for their love of being cooped up.

I ruled out a closet, and everywhere else I considered was way too big. I had bigger closets upstairs but I did not relish the thought of shutting her up in a closet upstairs for five weeks. Then I got an inspiration.

I put her in my little postage-stamp bathroom. It was bigger than a closet but wasn't so big where she would have room to have some movement. I first put down drop cloths all over the floor, enough that they were about knee deep to discourage any walking Honey Bunny may wish to do. I set up a small litter box, put in a food and water dish, and brought in Honey Bunny to her new place and shut the door.

After a day, I couldn't stand her being shut up in the bathroom all by herself. There had to be a better way. I opened the door and placed a piece of plywood across the lower part of the door. This way she could hear what was going on about the house and kind of be included in the day-to-day happenings.

After two days, I didn't like that setup either. From her position on the floor, she couldn't see anything except the hallway ceiling.

Then the idea bulb went on again in my gray matter. I replaced the plywood with an old storm-door window. Much better! Honey Bunny was still confined, but now she could see what was going on and see her roomies as they went up and down the hall and in and out of rooms.

For five weeks, Honey Bunny stayed there. She only had to crawl about six inches for food or water and about twelve inches for the litter box. All the big cloths on the floor were like deep snow, so she wasn't walking anywhere. Meanwhile, when I needed to get in the bathroom, I only had to straddle the windowpane and I was in.

Five weeks later, I gathered her up and back to the hospital in Akron we went. She was not looking well after five weeks of sitting, so before we left I combed and brushed her and prettied her up for her doctor visit. She was looking really good when we left.

We got to Akron and in to see her doctor. When I took her out of the carrier, she was walking! She wasn't walking normally but she was up on her hind legs and not dragging herself.

The doctors there said, "Sometimes that happens." They said she may continue to improve but will never be one hundred percent.

I was so happy as I took Honey Bunny home. I was happier still when I let her down in the house, her house, and did not have to confine her to the bathroom.

The veterinarians were right. Honey Bunny improved over time, but she was not like she was before. She did not return to one hundred percent. She now walks like a raccoon. She kind of waddles. But she is mobile. She also kind of runs and kind of jumps, and she goes up and down stairs.

Honey Bunny's health emergencies were not over yet. A few years after Honey Bunny's spinal stroke, she came into the room where I was sitting. She was huffing and puffing like she had just completed the Ironman competition, breathing very fast and deep.

What was this? I certainly didn't know. I watched her for about fifteen minutes, thinking if she was out of breath, she would soon slow down. She didn't.

Another late night trip to the emergency clinic. The doctor at the emergency clinic put her in an oxygen chamber and I had to leave her for the remainder of the night.

I returned at 7:00 AM (more missed work but same understanding boss) to get her. She was now breathing normally on her own. The doctor had taken x-rays of her and told me that she did not have full lung capacity in one lung. I knew that already from her time at the Akron hospital, as they did every test in the world on her. I took her to see Dr. Jackson, and then back home where things got back to normal.

Normal as far as can be expected. Now, whenever I hear Honey Bunny cough, my heart is in my mouth. She has a tendency to cough sometimes and she will cough repeatedly for about a minute. Every time she does, it scares me.

Honey Bunny's medical problems were still not over. About a year later, Honey Bunny seemed to be dizzy and would stagger slightly when she walked. "Hello, emergency clinic? It's me, Honey Bunny. I'm on my way to see you."

When we arrived at the clinic, they had the oxygen chamber all ready for her, in anticipation of her having the same problem as last time, but it was not needed.

The doctor examined her and chastised me for not mentioning Honey Bunny's eyes. He pointed out that the iris in each of Honey Bunny's eyes were different. One was big and one was small. I had not noticed this at all, so I couldn't tell the doctor how long she had exhibited that symptom. Different sizes of iris indicate a stroke, and I felt really badly like I had neglected something important in Honey Bunny's care.

The doctor took a body x-ray of Honey Bunny. There was nothing significant to indicate a stroke or causing her symptoms, but something totally out of left field showed up. On her x-ray, back toward her tail, she had two vertebrae fused together. Wow! Was this Honey Bunny's spinal stroke? Did she slip a disc as it happens with humans? Is that what had happened years ago during that awful time? Was her healing the fusing together of the vertebrae?

However, the doctor was no closer to a diagnosis for Honey Bunny's "stroke" and advised me to get her to my regular vet first thing. I was all set for another trip to Akron.

Back to the vet first thing, and more missed work. Dr. Jackson was not there that day. Dr. Jackson had been taking care of all of my animals since day one, and I had never had any of them with another vet. I didn't want to risk further harm to Honey Bunny by waiting a whole day for him to be back.

So Honey Bunny got to see another vet, Dr. Leung. While Dr. Leung was examining Honey Bunny, I mentioned that there was some crustiness on Honey Bunny's ear. Dr. Leung began checking and she got very concerned. She thought Honey Bunny could have an ear infection, and did the testing right there and found she did have an ear infection.

This was good news, maybe. Dr. Leung said that the infection could explain why Honey Bunny was staggering and seemed dizzy. She even told me it could explain Honey Bunny's eyes. She went on to explain that a cat's optic nerve wound around near where the ear infection was and if the infection was pressing on the optic nerve it could explain the difference in the size of each iris. Curing the infection *may* cause the eyes to return to normal. She sent us home with some medicine for Honey Bunny's ears and a return appointment.

I took Honey Bunny back to see Dr. Leung after ten days. The ear infection seemed to be healed, but her eyes were still the same. Dr. Leung had told me that Honey Bunny's eyes might not ever return to normal. But then again, they might.

About five weeks later, I was reading. As usual, Honey Bunny jumped up in my lap and crawled up my body to stick her nose in my face. This is very distracting when you are reading. But as she touched her cold nose to my nose, I looked her in the face and noticed both of her eyes were the same size. I set my book aside and looked and looked, and sure enough, each iris was the same size!

I ran for my camera and managed to get a decent shot showing each of her eyes. I emailed the photo it to Dr. Leung, who was very pleased, to say the least.

As of this writing, Honey Bunny is doing well. She is the den mother and goes around to each of the cats all day long to see how they are doing. Many times, I will see her snuggled up to one of the other cats. In fact, she will impose herself on the other cats, and often, they just want to be alone and they will get up and find somewhere else to snooze.

All except Kitty. Kitty does not like Honey Bunny. Even though Honey Bunny does everything she can to be friendly with Kitty. She will go by Kitty and plop down on her side next to Kitty in total submission. Kitty will hiss, growl, and walk away. Kitty does not like her. But Kitty does not particularly care for any of her roommates, either. But that's Kitty.

MY CATS - HONEY BUNNY

I have to relate another thing about Honey Bunny. This account just wouldn't be complete without including this. I hope you will bear with me on this.

As I related earlier, Honey Bunny was never one hundred percent after her spinal stroke that may not have been a spinal stroke. As I stated, she walks differently since then. This condition has also had some effect on her musculature, and as a consequence, things back there are not quite tight, not exactly one hundred percent. As a result of this, on some occasions, she leaves the litter box before she is done. She does not know this, though. Since this is a #2 condition and not #1, when this happens, it is relatively easy to clean up.

However, when Honey Bunny on occasion gets "runny," things are different. Instead of having to clean up a lump a few feet from the litter box, I have to clean up goo and Honey Bunny. As she is a long-haired cat, this gets real messy. This does not happen too often, but when it does, it always happens on the maid's day off and I have to clean her up.

The first time this happened, I had to corner her and forcibly take her to the bathroom. She was all messy and she knew it, and in her mind probably concluded that she did something wrong.

In the bathroom, I had to close the door so she couldn't get out. Then I proceeded to clean her up. She did not like it and growled and grumbled the entire time. These "runny" incidents usually last for about three days, so the next day I had to do the same—haul her into the bathroom and clean her up, and I got the same reaction from Honey Bunny.

On the third day, I was standing by the bathroom sink and she was at my feet. She got my attention because she kept swinging her butt sideways and hitting it against my leg. She kept doing this over and over. I finally figured out that she wanted something, and when I looked I saw that she needed a cleaning.

This has now become an almost daily routine. She comes in the bathroom and swings her rump into my leg. She then watches while I prepare a wet cleaning cloth and when I turn from the sink she plops down and rolls on her side so I can clean her.

As I said, the runny days where she actually needs to be cleaned are rare, but she has come to expect this almost every day. I marvel that an animal could be so concerned about its hygiene.

As Honey Bunny is now up in years, I thought she might like to go outside. She's always at the back door looking out so I decided to let her out if she wanted.

One nice day, I picked her up and took her outside. She got scared and began running toward the bushes. I don't know why she was scared. So I grabbed her and took her back inside.

After that, when she was at the door, I would hold the door open and talk to her, inviting her to come out if she wanted. Her response was to think about it. All the while, I was air conditioning the whole world.

She finally ventured out. She goes all of about two feet from the door. She will hide under the bush or eat grass. On some really rare days, she will trek over to the fence where there is catnip growing and indulge herself. Then it's back to the door where she will wail when she wants to go back into the house.

Honey Bunny's personal hygiene still amazes me after many years of having to clean her.

And she is still the social gadabout, going about the house daily and checking on all her roommates to see how they are and do a little nuzzling and grooming. Kitty of course does not appreciate this.

Honey Bunny adores attention. Any attention. She will never miss a chance for attention and will get on my lap as soon as she realizes I am sitting, and she is usually the first on the bed when I go to bed at night. Honey Bunny thinks nothing about butting in on any of the other cats that may be on my lap and she will muscle them out of the way so she can be on my lap. This usually results in hissing and growling from the displaced cat. Honey Bunny loves attention so much I am sure that I could sit in the corner and start stroking a shoe and she would soon show up to take the place of the shoe.

Strangest of all, Honey Bunny will pick up a soft cat toy in her mouth and take it somewhere. While walking with this toy in her mouth, she emits a really pitiful and heartbreaking sound. When she gets to where she is going she will drop the toy and stop the noise. I don't know what this is all about and my speculations about it are all sad.

As this goes to press, Honey Bunny still intimidates Kitty. Not intentionally; it's just the way she is. But she never gives up and still goes by Kitty trying to be friends. Honey Bunny still waddles more than walks and does not have full feeling in her back end. And she still comes to me for her almost daily "cleanups."

I have begun letting Honey Bunny outside more and more but only when I am there to watch her. And she will once in a while venture more than six feet from the door. Luckily, she does not have Kitty's yen to explore, so I do not need to watch her real closely.

My Cats - Honey Honey

You already know a little bit about Honey Honey from reading about Honey Bunny.

    I didn't see much of Honey Honey the first year she was here as she hid in the basement all day. I would only see her when she followed Honey Bunny up to the kitchen for food. Not knowing whether to run away or stop eating, she chose to keep eating, and thus, I would get to pet her while she ate.

In her early days, she thought the basement was entirely her domain and thus the situation with Kitty and the litter box, which I related. I have since then completed a refurb of my basement and now I spend time there and so do the other cats, so Honey Honey has come to know that the basement is not just her domain any more.

In the years since then she has explored the rest of the house, and her now second favorite hangout is the kitchen.

She has always been skittish around me but recently has come to realize that getting combed and brushed by her human is not such a bad thing. She is now comfortable anywhere in the house. Twice already, yes, twice she has actually come up on the bed when I was in it. The big break through just came when she jumped up on my chair while I was reading and spent time on my lap. Not much time, but for her this was quite a change in behavior.

Honey Honey's big adventure since she has been here was that she went missing for five days. This situation was one big comedy of errors, but I thank God it had a happy ending. Here's what happened.

Item A: I used to put uneaten cat food and table scraps out for the neighborhood cats. A better use than throwing it out. A few regulars would show up at night for these treats. One of the cats looked exactly like Honey Honey. (I have a photo.)

Item B: Honey Honey and Honey Bunny liked to sit on the windowsill of my upstairs rear window. (I have a photo.)

One afternoon, I got home and went to the front to get the mail. In the corner by the porch was the cat that looked like Honey Honey. I talked to it and tried not to scare it. Later that day, this cat was next to my garage. Once again, I talked to it and it did not seem frightened.

The next day, I realized I had not seen Honey Honey in a while. This was at the point in her time here when it was not uncommon for me to not see her for long periods. This time, I got an "uh-oh" feeling and I went looking for her. After a thorough search of the house, I determined that she was not in it.

How did she get out? I am always very careful when going outside so no cat gets sneaky and slips out before I can close the door. The only other exit was the window upstairs. It was easy for me to visualize Honey Honey sitting on the windowsill enjoying the view, and Honey Bunny coming along and wanting to be on the windowsill also.

I envisioned Honey Bunny jumping up to the windowsill and knocking Honey Honey out the window. There is grass beneath so a fall like that is nothing for a cat.

When I realized Honey Honey was missing, a mountain fell on me and I realized that the cat I had seen outside twice the day before was not the cat that looked like Honey Honey but was in fact Honey Honey.

Feeling like the biggest idiot in the world, I went outside looking for her. She was nowhere to be found. I searched around the neighborhood, calling out for her but to no avail. After three days, I gave up hope of ever seeing her again. At that time, I was convinced that if a cat didn't come back after three days, then it was gone for good.

Two days later was my birthday and the fifth day Honey Honey was missing. I had previously put in for the day off, and as a birthday present to myself, I was going to treat myself to a movie. I returned home from the movie in the early afternoon and when I got out of my vehicle, I saw Honey Honey next to the garage. She was back! Best birthday present ever!

Honey Honey does not sit on the windowsill anymore and I am glad. What I don't understand is that Honey Bunny no longer does either. Go figure.

This episode with Honey Honey did drive home something with me. Because Honey Honey was so standoffish with me, staying in the basement and never coming around all the time, I had never been able to bond with her. Because of that, I wondered if I loved her as I loved the other cats. Her returning home after five days made me realize how much I had missed her and how much I did love her. The bonding came later.

Early on in that bonding process, Honey Honey would run up and lie down on the steps halfway up from the basement. She did this when I was in the basement. This put her at eye level with me, with me standing on a lower step. One day, I petted her like that. So getting on that step became sort of a ritual in her early bonding with me. As long as she was even with my eyes, she was OK. But not so if I was standing over her.

On those basement steps petting sessions, I noticed that she drooled a great deal. I even called her a feline St. Bernard because of her drooling. Later, as our bonding increased and she became more comfortable around me and would get in my lap, I noticed that Honey Honey had no teeth! I was both amazed and concerned. Was it something I did? Or something I didn't do?

In any case, she was almost four by then, and there was nothing I could do about it. Her lack of teeth did not seem to hinder her eating at all, and she chowed down on any of the food I put out for the cats, including dry cat treats, which she loves as much as Oscar does.

So all was well as far as that, but it still leaves me wondering. Was she born without teeth? Did she get teeth and lose them after she came to stay with me? And if so, did it hurt? I will never know these answers.

The downside of Honey Honey not having her teeth is that she cannot groom herself. That's right, all you non-cat people, cats need their teeth for their grooming. I know all you non-cat people think that the cats are just licking themselves but that's not so. They are grooming their fur, and by using their front grooming teeth, they are able to keep out all the tangles and snags. This leaves Honey Honey one big mat of snags and tangles, which I do my best to fix up and keep her neat.

The only problem is Honey Honey has no patience for this, most likely due to the hair pulling involved, and will not let me work on her for more than three or four minutes. On the other hand, Honey Bunny, who rarely gets a tangle even though her hair is just as long, will sit in my lap for hours while I comb and brush her. Such is the life of a cat.

There have been no more adventures involving Honey Honey. Like the others, she gets mellower with age. She has been low maintenance, and I am eternally grateful that she has not had the medical problems of her aunt or the other critters.

Honey Honey typically still stays off by herself, usually in the basement or some other place where it is cool. I surmise this is due to her thick fur, so she is just more comfortable where it is cooler.

I think she still thinks Honey Bunny is her mother, and she is frequently curled up with her enjoying a nap.

Honey Honey, after her many years of staying mostly in the basement, has finally joined the rest of the group and interacts with the rest of us in all the rooms of the house.

She has even ventured all the way to the bedroom and came up onto the bed at night. My ego naturally thought it was so she could be with me. Further evaluation made me realize she just comes onto the bed to be with Honey Bunny.

She continues to climb onto my lap for a few minutes of attention once in a while. When she does, I grab for the comb and scissors and get in a few minutes of grooming before she gets mad and leaves.

My Cats - Pierre

One fall evening, two friends were visiting. We were in the garage, drinking beer and listening to the baseball game. It was about 10:00 PM. As we were yakking, I noticed a cat materialize out of the darkness, coming up the driveway toward the garage. I had never seen this cat before and I couldn't figure out what it was up to. I figured all the talking, the lights glaring, and the radio playing would make it shy away back into the darkness.

Still it came up the driveway and into the garage! It circled around the garage and around all of us. Then it went back down the driveway and back the way it came. After a few minutes, one of the guys asked if that was one of my cats. I had never seen it before.

And I didn't see it again for a while. Then I saw it again. Then it went away for a while. This went on for about four of these cycles. The cat was a big Tom, and I was sure he was someone's pet because he was so friendly. He didn't look gaunt and hungry like a stray. I thought he was only coming around to snack on the food that I put out to feed the strays.

As time went by, he began hanging around longer and longer until he finally he took up residence in my garage. He got up into the rafters. He stayed there all winter, and he was fed along with the other strays that came around.

This cat was amazing. A full-grown unaltered male, affectionate as all get out. He had all the qualities of a good house pet. He was a hand flipper, a head bumper, and an ankle eighter. The other cats could see him from the kitchen window and the back door. There seemed to be no anxiety with any of the cats about him like there is when a strange cat comes around. Several times, I held open the door to see if he would come in, but he didn't.

I named him Pierre. I named him after the owner of a deli I have frequented for many years. Besides making great sandwiches the owner, Pierre, had been giving me meat scraps to feed the strays. So I thought it would be appropriate to name this cat after the man who had been feeding him all this time.

One day, when I was putting out food before leaving for my job, he didn't show up as he usually did. I called and I heard him meowing from up in the rafters. I could see him up there, but he wouldn't come down. He always came down when I showed up. I got my ladder and climbed up to discover he was hurt. Something was wrong with his leg. He couldn't or wouldn't stand on it. I scooped him up and called work to say I would be late and off we went to see Dr. Jackson. I asked Dr. Jackson to neuter Pierre while he was there. I didn't consult Pierre on this matter.

Since I now had money invested in Pierre, I invested in an ID collar for him that had my phone number on it. After these many months, I still believed he was someone's pet and that someone might be looking for him. Now he had my collar on and was missing some anatomy. I was sure that if he were someone's pet, I would soon be getting a phone call. That call never came, and soon, Pierre was an everyday fixture in the garage with no more occasional absences.

After living in my garage all winter, I decided to make Pierre one of the family and let him in the house with the other cats, but he wouldn't come in. He would stand there like a big dummy when I was holding the door open for him, but he wouldn't come in. Finally, I picked him up and carried him in.

I first took him to the basement where the litter box was so he would know where that was in case he felt the need. The other cats gathered around to stare and sniff at him. No growls, hisses, or paw swiping. It was good.

Pierre did not act like any cat I have ever brought home. Pierre acted as if he was home. Instead of heading for a corner to hide, he circled around the same way he had that first day in the garage. He acted as if he had been here before. He gave a few sniffs to things in the area and then went upstairs and went to the food bowls. He went right to them. After a snack, he roamed the house checking things out. Again, acting as if he had been here before.

That night, he came on the bed and slept next to my head all night, displacing Schiz from his place.

So now, I had six cats, Kitty, Schiz, Oscar, Honey Bunny, Honey Honey, and Pierre.

Pierre continues to amaze me. One night, I got up about 3:00 AM to get something to drink from the refrigerator. I looked out the window and there was Pierre with six other cats sitting in front of my garage. No fighting, no posturing, and no wailing challenges. It looked like some sort of moonlight cat convention.

One of Pierre's amazing actions occurred early on. It happened when Schiz died. Knowing what would be coming and the time of the year, I had already prepared a burial place for Schiz several days before.

On an early March Saturday afternoon, I buried him. Pierre had been outside all the while I was attending to this. He was doing his thing and roaming all around. After I finished the burial, I got a lawn chair and set it by the grave. I sat there talking to God and remembering Schiz. Pierre came over and jumped up on my lap. He

MY CATS - PIERRE

nestled down and put his head up under my chin, and just stayed there.

As we sat there, the wind picked up and big snowflakes began coming down. Pierre sat with me the whole time. We stayed there for about thirty minutes until the weather began to get the best of me and we both went inside.

One night, I went out to the garage to feed Scaredy, and Pierre came with me. I was doing my thing with the food and I saw movement down by my feet out of the corner of my eye. Thinking it was Pierre, I continued until a moment later I saw Pierre about four feet away from me, staring at something by me. I looked down and it was a skunk! Right by my feet! Not Pierre.

I had seen skunks in the backyard many times but never this close and personal. I made a quick sidestep away from the skunk and then a quick exit from the garage.

There was a television show titled *Everybody Loves Raymond*. That is how Pierre is—everybody and everything loves him. He gets along with all his indoor roommates and with people who visit me. Various animals show up in my garage: cats, raccoons, possum, and skunks. Pierre and Scaredy get along with all of them. The proof? No wounds, no scratches, and no animal fur left around. Besides, I have pictures.

Pierre has never been sprayed by a skunk even though my neighbor and the previous neighbor both had their dogs sprayed. Pierre has never come home injured so I know he is not mixing it up with these other critters. Some years ago, a possum took up residence in the garage for the entire winter and they all got along. I even got the possum box trained.

Raccoons have come around once and a while. The cats get along with them but they bother me. Besides the mess they make in my garage they can be vicious. And they can have rabies. I haven't figured out how to keep the raccoons out while allowing other critters in.

One day, I noticed Pierre's tail was not looking right. It was just hanging. Hanging down and to the left. I couldn't find any injuries and he didn't show any distress when I poked and prodded his tail and rear to see if he was injured.

But his tail just hung there, not up in the air, not straight out, and not straight down. Just hanging to the left. After four days of this, I took him to Dr. Jackson. Dr. Jackson was unable to find any cause as to why Pierre's tail was hanging; there were no injuries, sprains, or breaks. Since there was nothing apparent to be treated or medicated, I took Pierre home.

Then, over about four weeks, his tail gradually came back to life. Over a few weeks, it came up to horizontal, then came up higher, but still to the left. Eventually, it returned to normalcy of being up, down, or straight back, depending on Pierre's anxiety level.

Pierre still goes outside. It has been some years since he went missing (See *Pierre & Scaredy's Not So Excellent Adventure*), and once in a while, he is not there when I expect him. When this happens, I immediately transition to my nervous-wreck mode until he comes back. There is no waiting period when he is missing. I just go from normal calmness to complete hysteria when he is not here when he should be.

As this goes to press, Pierre doesn't go out as much anymore and much prefers to enjoy the air conditioning on hot days and the heater outlets on winter days. I guess he is like most of us—he is older and wiser and the great outdoors doesn't hold as much appeal as in younger days.

Pierre is always by my ankles. He tweaks his way in and out of my legs doing figure eights when he is excited about something and I am walking. I worry that I will inadvertently kick him or step on him. There have been close calls already. I also worry that someday I will trip over him. I have told a few friends that if I am ever found dead of a fall, it will be because of Pierre and his closeness.

My other cats can walk around on my desk, the table, shelves, or anything without stepping on anything—very graceful just like a cat should be. Not Pierre. He can't walk on my desk without walking right on my keyboard and anything else. He will just plow through or across anything in his way. He is like that anywhere else in the house. That's when I sometimes refer to him as "Big Clunk."

One of Pierre's attributes that I don't understand is his voice. For such a big huge lump of a cat, he has the quietest voice of any cat I've had. When he's at the back door and howls to be let in, I can't hear him unless I am very close to the door. Yet I can hear Honey Bunny howling to be let in from just about anywhere.

But he is an almost twenty pounds of big loveable feline fun and companionship.

My Cats - Scaredy

Scaredy showed up sometime in late 2006 or early 2007. I can't remember when I first noticed her. My first photo of her is dated February 2007. I officially named her Scaredy Cat in November 2008.

What separated her from the other strays is that she hung around the place. After a while, I noticed she seemed to be waiting around for Pierre to come outside. As time went by, I found this to be true.

She adores him and is always waiting for him to come out. I use the word adores in the way a human adores another human as I don't know what animal term applies to the way Scaredy hangs around and dotes on Pierre.

Before she began hanging around, I don't know where she stayed. I don't know if she was feral, wild, or a stray. Early on, she would sit on top of the back fence next door and wait for Pierre. Back then, if I came to the door and looked out, she would run away. I had to sneak a peek through a window to see her, and if she saw me, she took off to hide.

It took months and months and months, but over time, she would come closer and not run away if she saw me. I could never get more than six feet from her, but eventually, she would not run if she saw me as long as I stayed my distance.

Scaredy brought forth four litters of kittens that I know of. Where she had her first, I don't know; but when they got older, she brought them to my garage as kittens. Why not, that's where the food was. The kittens took up residence beneath the hood of my pickup truck. My neighbor Stacy, who lives in the house behind me, helped get homes for them.

Scaredy's second litter was born elsewhere but she brought them to my garage when they were only as big as my thumb. She was forced out of wherever she birthed them by heavy rain. I set up a nest for her, and as the kittens grew up, Stacy once again helped me find homes for them.

Her third litter was actually born in my garage in early winter. I had a nest already built for her by the time she was ready, and this time she had them in my garage. Stacy helped me find homes for them, again. In fact, she took kittens from all the litters for herself. I now thought of her as Saint Stacy, and her house as Saint Stacy's home for unclaimed cats.

All these kittens were vibrant and healthy and I attribute that to Scaredy's good diet she had during her pregnancies and not having to hunt and scavenge for garbage. However, I had to do something about her penchant for bringing forth more life in my garage!

I bought a trap on the Internet and planned to catch her and take her to Dr. Jackson to get her fixed. I had previously told him that one day I would be bringing in a cat for neutering, and I would be bringing it in with no prior appointment and not to be surprised.

Around that time, a raccoon had moved into the garage, and I had to figure out how to get rid of it. I wanted to trap Scaredy, not some raccoon. Meanwhile, time was running out because Scaredy was almost ready to wean the kittens and I had not wanted to trap her before she weaned her kittens.

By the time I got rid of the raccoon and made all the arrangements, Scaredy was pregnant again. She had the forth litter that I know of somewhere else, but once again, heavy rains encouraged her to bring the kittens into my garage. Five more little worms about the size of my thumb! I set up her nest again, moved the kittens into it, and waited for them to grow up.

I didn't want Saint Stacy to know that I had another litter I would need to find homes for; I just couldn't impose on her again. As the kittens got of age to be away from their mom, I found homes for four of the kittens. Each person who took a kitten happened along by accident! People wanting a kitten just appeared in my life at just that right time.

Out came the trap again and the arrangements were made with Dr. Jackson, and when the time was right, I set the trap. I caught Scaredy the first try, and a day later, she was all fixed up! No more kittens.

Dr. Jackson told me she had been pregnant again. I was sad to hear that but it was done already. I could only hope that she would not know this, and somehow be changed because of it. I also had her vaccinated for rabies.

I kept Scaredy in the house for three weeks after the surgery. This was so I could give her the pain medication Dr. Jackson had prescribed for her. Of course, Scaredy had other ideas and just like outdoors, I couldn't get near her.

I didn't go looking for her while she was indoors. I didn't want her to feel in danger or intimidated. I was truly hoping she would become accustomed to being indoors during her stay. But she never came out when I was around and I was never able to give her the pills. I felt terrible, imagining the pain she must have experienced while healing from her surgery.

My hope that Scaredy would become used to house living didn't seem to be working out, as she stayed hidden whenever I was around. She obviously came out when I was not around because she had to eat and she was using the litter box.

Scaredy obviously was not happy, and after about three weeks, it was getting to me. So one evening, I shut the bedroom door and opened the window, and an hour later, she was gone from inside the house. The next morning, she was outside waiting for me to bring her food just like always.

Now that I had spent loads of money on Scaredy, I told myself she was officially mine even if she did live in the garage. Scaredy was cat number seven.

Seven? Didn't I say I was up to five cats? Where did number six come from, you ask?

I had managed to find homes for four of Scaredy's last litter. After trapping Scaredy to take her to the vet, there was still one last kitten needing a home. I couldn't very well leave this last kitten out in the garage without her mom, could I? So that's where cat number six came from. She was the last cat from Scaredy's last litter, so I brought her in to join the rest of the group. After a month, I named her Sweetie Sweets and I call her Sweetie.

After these many years, Scaredy is no longer afraid of me but she is still leery. I can get a few feet from her, and of course, I am unable to pet her. That doesn't stop her from showing up at the back door and scolding me when she is hungry. She just chats and chatters until I bring out food for her. Sometimes, when she is really hungry, she will come within about a foot, meowing up a storm at me about whatever is on her mind. But if I reach out a hand—no, no, and she scampers away.

When winter approached, I made up a sleeping nest for Scaredy. It was a place draped in shipping quilts and off the cement floor.

There she can hide when I come around, and find shelter from the wind when I have to open the big door.

I was always concerned because Scaredy's water and food was freezing. On really cold days, the food and water would freeze really fast. This was really bothering me, so I got Scaredy a heater. A nifty patio heater. It is an infrared heater and gives off a soft pink light as it emits warmth. I have it suspended in the back corner where her nest and food are located. I hooked it to a thermostat and it comes on at about thirty degrees and stays on until the temperature goes above forty degrees. Now her food and water don't freeze, and she has warmth on those real cold and windy days.

I also got Scaredy an electric water fountain-drinking dish. The same one as I had got for the inside cats. They liked it, used it, and drank more than they did out of a bowl. So now, Scaredy has her own heated apartment with running water. How's that for a stray? Pierre gets to benefit from it too whenever he goes outside into the nasty weather.

As this goes to press, Scaredy still lives in the garage. She still won't let me touch her, but sometimes, if I hold out my hand and extend my finger she will come over and sniff it. A far cry from the early days when she would run away if I just appeared at the back door.

She chatters at scolds me, mostly at feeding time. I sure wish I knew what she is yakking about.

Sometimes, when she is preoccupied with Pierre or food, I sneak a touch. She quickly moves away and gives me one of her "how dare you" looks. I guess that is progress.

She still waits in all weather for Pierre to come out so she can be with him. Again, I don't have the words to describe her attachment to him. She waits and waits for him to come outside, sitting under the bush outside the back door. She'll be there in the crummiest weather, waiting to see if her Pierre is coming out. When Pierre does come out her reaction (joy?) is clearly visible. She meows and rubs herself against Pierre over and over.

It is hard to describe the attachment she has to Pierre without using human terms. I know she has no concept of love or devotion to Pierre or any idea that she misses him when he is inside. I know she does not know of the meaning of the happiness or joy that she has when the door opens and Pierre comes out.

I use human terms to describe the way Scaredy acts when she is around her beloved Pierre. Whatever it is that she feels for Pierre, it is something special, and seeing it myself gives me feelings of great wonder.

Pierre & Scaredy's Not so Excellent Adventure

About a week after the day when I opened my bedroom window and let Scaredy out of the house after her surgery, I noticed that Pierre hadn't come home. One day became two days. On the third day, I realized it was not only Pierre who had not come home but Scaredy was not around either.

I was perplexed. I didn't know what to do. *Both* of them gone? After a few more days, I came to the conclusion that the two of them must have gotten shut up in a building. What else would explain two cats missing at the same time? Unless, of course, they had come to some more sinister fate, which I didn't want to even think about.

After two weeks, I was at a loss. In fact, I was devastated. Pierre and Scaredy were still gone. Then one day at work, I read on the Internet a news article about a lady in Cincinnati who got her cat back after hiring a pet detective. Pet detective? I thought that *Pet Detective* was only a movie.

I searched the Internet to find that pet detectives really exist. After exhaustive searching, I located one. It was the same one from the news article! He was also the closest pet detective to where I lived. Except he couldn't get to me until the weekend!

In any case, things are what they are and by the magic of my credit card, the deal was sealed. He promised he would be at my place on Saturday. By that time, Pierre and Scaredy had been gone seventeen days. Worse yet, the temperature had dropped to five above zero.

The pet detective was Jim Berns, and he brought an assistant, two bloodhounds and about fourteen large "Missing Cats" signs.

The first thing was putting up the signs. It was five degrees out, and the wind was blowing about a thousand miles an hour. Two days previous, it had been in the forties!

Jim enlisted me to help hang the signs. That's the last thing I wanted to do. I wanted to sit in my house and be miserable while he solved my problem. But I knew where all the streets were into and out of my area so I helped.

He put up signs at every possible entrance or exit from my area. Coming in or going out of the area, these signs would be seen. And they were big signs. Not a piece of paper.

After we completely surrounded my neighborhood with the signs, he began going door to door with the bloodhounds. They got an immediate hit on a trail two houses away from me. It was a strong hit, but there was only one problem. There was a gate across the driveway and Mr. Berns informed me that he was not legally permitted to enter a yard with a closed gate without permission, and no one was home.

In addition, I had two boys from across the street going house to house putting flyers in the mailboxes. Further, I had contracted with a company that would make five thousand phone calls to all the listed phone numbers in my area, advising people to be on the lookout for my cats.

By the time Mr. Berns left to return to Cincinnati, the whole area was aware of my missing cats. Soon, I began to get phone calls but none of the leads panned out. And the weather remained brutally cold.

I began to include something different in my prayers. Nightly, I would focus very hard and I would say, "I believe in God, and I believe in miracles." Just those words. Nothing more.

Three weeks went by and nothing. Christmas came and went, and I hardly noticed it. New Year's holiday came and went. That had been my worst holiday season ever.

As time went by, I kept up my "I believe in God, and I believe in miracles" prayer. Being honest here, I have to say that one part of me kept saying too much time had passed, that there was no way Pierre and Scaredy could still be living, considering the brutal cold spell and no food. But another part of me kept focused, and I kept saying my short prayer. Even as the missing cats were approaching thirty days of being gone.

One call I did get was from Jaime Anton, a reporter from the local *News Sun* newspaper. She had seen the signs and was curious because it said "missing cats." Cats, plural. She had never seen a missing pet sign that had more than one missing pet listed. I explained the situation and Jamie wrote an article about Pierre and Scaredy and said it would be in that week's edition.

One day, I answered another call from my answering machine. It was a message from a lady who said my cats were in her garage. I called her back immediately. My first question was if they were still alive. She described them to a T, including Pierre's collar. Then the bomb came – she lived two houses away from me. The same house where the bloodhounds got their strongest hit and had the gate closed and no one was at home!

She went on to explain that they hardly ever used the garage. But her daughter had gone out to get their sled, and lo and behold, she saw two cats. She told her mother and the mother called me, but by the time I got the call, she was at her job. I would have to wait until after 4:00 PM the next day to get Pierre. But the lady had put some cat food in the garage so they had finally got to eat. Pierre and Scaredy had been gone thirty days at this time.

I got home from work at 4:00 PM the next day. As anxious as I was to get Pierre, the first thing I did was to put food and water out in the garage for Scaredy. Then I rushed two houses over. The lady let me into the backyard and opened the people door on the garage. I went in and couldn't see Pierre anywhere. I thought he would be up in the rafters like he did when he lived in my garage, but this garage had the rafters hidden by a ceiling, and I couldn't see beyond that ceiling. How did the cats get up there? I asked the lady, and she pointed to a hole in the back corner over the top of an old bedroom dresser. I asked her to leave me alone in the garage and I softly called out to Pierre like I always did.

Nothing. I called out again and again and again. It seemed like hours but was about a minute when I finally heard a teeny-tiny meow. I called again and again, another meow. I couldn't see where it was coming from. This went on several times, but the meow was getting louder each time. Then I looked and there was Pierre sitting on top of that old dresser. I had not seen him come down from where ever he was in the rafters. He wasn't there and then there he was.

I coaxed him down, as he was about seven feet up on top of the dresser. I could see his collar hanging loosely around his neck. He came down into my arms and I held him to me and exited the garage. He smelled like greasy rags.

The lady and her daughter were outside with big smiles on their faces. I walked past and asked her to leave the door open for a while. I hadn't seen Scaredy, but I knew if there were no people around she would come out and return home.

I took Pierre home and set him down in the kitchen. All the other cats came by and after a sniff of him, they all gave him a hiss. Since he smelled like a moldy grease rag. I guess they weren't totally sure whom he was. I knew he was hungry and he did eat some food but what surprised me was how much water he drank. Three times over the next half hour, he went to the water and drank lots and lots of water.

Scaredy came back just as I expected and was in my garage as usual for her. These two cats had been locked up for thirty-one days with no food or water. And I had them back alive and seemingly no worse for the experience. I never actually cried until the day after they were back. It took that long to sink in as to how close it was and that it was all over.

Also, my story in the *News Sun* newspaper came out that same day.

I notified Jaime at the *News Sun* newspaper and told her that the cats were back home safe and sound. She interviewed me and interviewed my neighbor lady and her daughter, and the next week a follow-up article with the happy ending was printed in the *News Sun* newspaper.

The end to this story was me going around cutting down all the "missing cats" signs. What a contrast in human emotion. Putting them up, I was about as miserable as a person could be; two of my cats were gone and I was devastated and the temperature had been five degrees. On the day I was taking them down, it was sunny and warm and I was on top of the world. My cats were home. I was sunny and warm.

Here are the URL links to the two stories in the *News Sun* about Pierre and Scaredy being lost and then found.

http://blog.cleveland.com/newssun/2009/01/man_hires_detective_to_find_mi.html

http://blog.cleveland.com/newssun/2009/01/cats_lost_on_muskingum_are_saf.html

My Cats ~ Sweetie

As I related, Sweetie was the last kitten from the last litter from her mother, Scaredy. I brought her into the house and into the family the day I trapped her mother and took her to get her reproductive zeal readjusted.

I brought Sweetie in from the garage where she had been raised and put her in the house with the rest of crew. Everything went well—no hissing, howls, or fights. She fit right in and was soon exploring the house at 50 mph. Kitty, of course, did not care to see yet another cat coming in to her world.

Sweetie is a sweetie. As Kitty is my senior citizen, Sweetie is my baby. She is full-grown but she has her mother's small stature, and next to the other horses I have running around here, she looks like a kitten.

Sweetie fits in well, and in the beginning she played with Oscar a lot, which I really liked since Oscar never had much of a life here as a kitten and never had a playmate.

Sweetie, just like her mother, adores Pierre. I constantly find her with him. It is quite amusing to see great big Pierre crammed into a basket or box and Sweetie trying to climb in with him. Usually, Pierre gets mad and stalks off, but sometimes, she is successful. Then it's like twenty-five pounds of fur in a twenty-pound container. Their coloring is so similar that when they are together they look like one big fur ball.

Sweetie gets along with the other cats and will take a swipe at Kitty once in a while. Kitty, of course, doesn't care for her.

If nature runs its course normally, I figure that in ten years it will be just Sweetie and me. Kitty is now over seventeen and the others are not far behind. And there is no stopping the natural cycle of life and death. When the time comes, and it is only Sweetie and me, I will evaluate if I will take on or can take on another cat. Sweetie will be old by then, and I, too, will be just a tad older.

Sweetie is a real blessing. I still don't have her mom in the house (yet) but I have her. She looks a lot like her mom and she is a real delight. She is so full of energy. She is very vocal and always giving me a piece of her mind.

Sweetie likes chip dip, and whenever I have some, she stands on my arm and samples it.

She continues to scold me all the time for all sorts of infractions such as lack of attention and low levels of food in the kitty dish.

Just like her mom.

Other cats no longer in my life but always in my heart

You've read about my seven miracle cats, but you don't know about the cats in my life leading up to, and overlapping, the time involving those seven cats.

This is relevant to what you have already read about.

Kiddee—You were my first try at having a pet cat. I got you from a barn full of cats out in the country. Our time was short because you were sick. I still see you in my mind that very last time. Please forgive me.

Funny Face—You were a great big guy with a funny face that could jump off my second floor balcony to go explore. I got you from the shelter but you too were sick. Please forgive me.

Lunch—We were both young and bulletproof. We both enjoyed the best that life threw at us. You were big and bad and you protected your territory ferociously. I know because I remember all the trophies you left for me at the back door. And then, you would sit still for me on the sink while I picked off your scabs and cleaned all your battle wounds, never flinching or complaining, knowing that I was helping you.

After eight years of good companionship, kidney failure took you.

I remember that I was devastated. How could it be? You were my great big cat buddy, and life was great and then you were gone. I woke up then. Life is great but life does not go on forever.

Baby—Ah, my gentle little mostly Siamese cuddle Baby. Everybody, and I mean everybody, took a liking to you and your distinctive vocalizations, and you took to everybody too. You were a lap cat, an under-the-covers sleeping buddy, and you would many times stand guard in the bathroom while I bathed.

I got you to be a companion for Lunch. You were grown when I got you and you hung in with me for eighteen years, giving Lunch your company while I was away and giving me love, comfort, and companionship.

Pee—My South American Margay jungle tree cat. You were so abused by those I bought you from, but I didn't know it until later. You were a grand and beautiful feline. How I regret that I couldn't take care of you properly after all the abuse you had endured. It broke my heart to give you up, but I knew it was for your benefit.

Memphis Kitty—A fuzzy white ball of stray kitten found by the bridge from Memphis, Tennessee to West Memphis, Arkansas. What a delight playing with you for those few days. I have regretted ever since that I did not bring you home. I pray your life turned out well.

Flea Bag—You walked from across the street, up my driveway, across my front walk, and then up on my porch. When I opened the door, you came right into the house. I had never seen you before.

You stayed with me a while but I had this incorrect idea that I could not take care of three cats, so I took you to my sister's place in the country. There, you lived with many other cats and animals, and had a good life.

Spook—I did not want to experience what I had gone through with Kiddee and Funny Face. When I called the shelter I asked if they had a cat that they knew positively had previous medical care and shots. You were there because your previous human couldn't have an animal in their apartment, and you had a medical record. I took you home confident that you wouldn't get sick in a few weeks.

I got you after the passing of Lunch to be a companion for Baby. It was coincidence that you looked just like Lunch, and it was fun watching neighbors and friends realize that you weren't Lunch.

Your previous human had declawed you and I was astounded one day when my neighbor said you were in his tree trying to see into the birdhouse. I thought he was mistaken until I saw it too. But I have a photo of you in that tree trying to peer into the little hole in the front of the birdhouse.

When I got you, I took you home, confident that you wouldn't get sick in a few weeks. I took you to the vet regularly and made sure you all your vaccinations were up to date. An exercise in futility as feline leukemia took you away too soon.

Mr. Nosey—I brought you home from the county fair to fill in the blank left by the passing of Spook. The old bippy next door named you and I let it stand. But you were no nosier than any other curious cat. You stayed awhile with me for a few years, and then one day, you never came home. I pray that you did not run into trouble and that you had a good life.

Microcat—I named you Microcat because I got you from the grounds of the company I worked for at the time. The company's name was Microtek, and so I named you Microcat. Everyone just called you Mike.

I had been out of town on business, and when I got back, you were making yourself at home in the shrubbery in front of the building. I was told you had been there for two days. We all assumed your owner had abandoned you from the big apartment complex nearby.

I took you home and got to experience firsthand the terrible results of what happens when a house cat is abandoned. My heart broke when you vomited up live round worms and tapeworms. I got you to see Dr. Jackson fast and those problems were dealt with in a big hurry.

But that was not the end. Dummy me, when I first brought you home I just waltzed you into the house and plopped you down. Wrong move! You had fleas. Really bad.

Within weeks, the entire house was infested, including poor Baby, who was up in years by this time and was miserable. My ankles looked like I had some kind of pox. But we got through all that, and you were a great and wonderful cat all the way until you passed.

Rough Tough Phlough - You were a big orange ugly cat living in my neighbor's unused garage, living life as a stray after you had been abandoned when your human moved away.

I had always thought I was a bigtime cat lover until you came along and showed me what a complete and utter hypocrite I was and had been.

However, I warmed to you and began putting food out for you. I remember that went on for a while because you wore a path from the side door of that garage to the back corner of my house on your visits to get the food I was putting out for you.

But winter arrived and when the temperature dripped below zero for several days in February, I brought you into the house.

The other cats wanted no part of you in the house with them. We tried everything. but it was all teeth and claws. I set you up in a separate room for a few weeks until the weather warmed up again.

How I remember how it was breaking my heart when I was carrying you back out into the cold, to have to go back to the garage. It must have broken your heart too because you bit me.

This tale had a happy ending! My boss where I was working at the time agreed that we needed a "warehouse cat."

After I took you to your new home, I took you to the vet just up the street and they kept you for a while and got you all fixed up and cleaned up. You took to your new home in the warehouse and everyone at work took to you. Even though you were all cleaned up, you were still a big orange fur ball. And ugly. But you were as friendly and loving as anyone could ever hope a cat could be, and for that everyone loved you.

When I left that job for greener pastures, I sent them a check for expenses for your continued care and feeding. They sent it back. They were that happy to have you.

Then one of the ladies who worked there knew a person who had lost her cat and was seeking a replacement, so you ended up in a real home after all. I found this out when they sent me a photo of you along with a letter informing me of your new dwelling.

Other Cats no longer in My Life - Angel

This is about a very remarkable experience with a kitten I had and has a bearing on the subject matter of this narrative.

I lost Angel after only two months under tragic circumstances; and to this day, it still hurts me to think about her. But I want to tell you about an extraordinary event surrounding her passing. To honor her memory, I will give you a brief summary of her time with me before she passed.

Having Angel meant I went from two cats to three cats and losing her meant I was back to two cats.

In October 2003, a small kitten wandered into our shop at work and got in behind a bunch of steel and was afraid to come out (exactly as I related to you about how I got Oscar). All day long, it mewed. In the afternoon, Jim got it—her—out and put her in a box. She was a small silver black kitten.

I thought about bringing her home, but as it turned out one of the guys at work, Corbin, said he would take it home. He and his wife had two cats already.

Things didn't work out right for them, and right before Thanksgiving, Corbin's wife called me and asked, practically begged, if I would take the kitten off their hands. She said it was too playful and kept chasing her other cats and they didn't like it. I said I would give it a try to see if she could blend in at my house.

I brought her home right after Thanksgiving and let her out, and she promptly ran off into the vast confines of the house. Over the next four weeks, I only had glimpses of her as she explored her new house and avoided me. I let her alone and she would eat when I wasn't around. After about two weeks, I could hear her at night with my other cats. Evidently, things were working out because I didn't hear any screeching or cat fights.

After another week, she started letting herself be seen by me but still wouldn't come around me. I just left her alone.

On Christmas day, while I was eating my dinner, and my other two cats were snoozing, I looked over and Angel was sitting about four feet away and watching me. I tossed her a piece of turkey. After that, things started improving. Within two weeks, she had taken over the house and was my bestest buddy.

She would chase Schiz, but he, being older, would just hiss and go away from her. But she was getting on well with Kitty, and Kitty was getting on well with her, to my surprise. Remember I related what an antisocial Kitty is? She doesn't care for any of the other cats.

In fact, Kitty and Angel would play for hours—usually at breakneck speeds through the house. Schiz and Kitty had definitely accepted Angel, so I began to think of a name for her. I tried *Noel* because she had come out on Christmas day. After about a week, I decided that name just didn't roll. I still wanted to name her something to do with Christmas so I named her Angel. That worked!

Angel carried things all over my house. Items from my workbench I found in the back bedroom. Items from upstairs I found downstairs. I even found stuff in the deep sink in the basement. Once I looked at her and she was headed down the hall toward the bedroom with a plastic spoon in her mouth.

She got into my candy and there were Lifesavers, not in the wrappers, all over the house. And she did all this together with Kitty, who had become quite attached to her—they had become great companions. Remember this for later.

I took Kitty in to see Dr. Jackson on January 8, and while there, I told him about Angel and that I needed to get her a checkup, shots, etc., and to get her spayed. He arranged to have me drop her off Thursday the 22nd and pick her up Saturday morning, the 24th. Dr.

Jackson did caution me that he did not normally take in an animal to do surgery on without previously having seen it for a complete exam. I persevered, mainly because I was trying to save the cost of an extra visitation.

Thursday at 5:00 PM, I had her at the vet. Like any pet, she was upset about going to the doctor. Everybody at the vet liked her and Dr. Jackson said she looked good. He said I could pick her up Saturday before noon.

On Friday at 10:15 AM, I was answering the phones at work and I received a call from Dr. Jackson. He told me that Angel had died. He said he tried everything to revive her but it was not to be.

At that time, I had been having a run of unfortunate luck with other things in my life. This was just too much for me. I left work and went home.

I went straight to my bedroom and was grieving over Angel. I called my friend Susan and blubbered the bad news to her. Susan tried her best to comfort me but to no avail. I was really affected by the news about Angel.

So I was in my room crying and blubbering for about twenty minutes when I noticed Schiz approaching me very slowly. He sensed something was not right, and when I called him, he came right to me. I petted him and enjoyed having him near me at this time.

After a few minutes of getting comforted by Schiz, I realized that I had not seen Kitty. In fact, I had not seen Kitty at all since I got home. I called for her but no Kitty.

Where was she? She's always around. I went looking all over, in all of her usual comfy spots. No Kitty. After about fifteen minutes, I caught a glimpse of her head poking out from behind the couch in the living room. She never went behind the couch! I called her but she went back behind the couch.

I looked behind the couch and Kitty was all hunkered down, crouching, and clearly, she was disturbed by something. Was it my blubbering that upset her? After all, she had never experienced me acting like that before.

I was finally able to coax her out after a while but she was still apprehensive about something. She was acting very cautiously, all crouched down on her belly with her tail tucked beneath her. Add to that her head was going back and forth, back and forth, like radar, looking all around.

I comforted her and after about five minutes she slowly came into the room some more, but she was still all hunched down with her belly right on the floor, and still looking all around. A minute or two more and I had coaxed her almost as far as the hallway.

I thought about picking her up, but since I had never seen her acting like this I didn't want to chance upsetting her more and being on the receiving end of her claws.

She came forward a few more steps still looking back and forth, back and forth. She was staring intensely down the hallway toward the back bedroom and still all hunkered down.

Suddenly, she did like a bird dog and fixed her stare straight into the back bedroom. Her head was no longer going back and forth. Her eyes were then locked in on to something. It was like I had seen my cats do when they spotted a bird. Only Kitty was locked on to something in the back bedroom.

Then, even more perplexing, she began walking backward. She didn't turn around; she walked straight back, backing up while maintaining her low profile with her belly low and her tail up tight. And she was still staring at some spot in the back bedroom.

She had backed up until she was almost at the couch. I was with her, petting her, and soothing her, and for the life of me, I was unable to see what she was staring at. Kitty stopped going backward and then remained frozen in position, tensed up, and staring at that something back there in the back room. Staring at something I was unable to see. This went on for at least two minutes.

Then, suddenly, Kitty relaxed. Just like that. She stood up, her tail came up, she turned around, and strolled into the kitchen to the food bowl. So nonchalantly. As if nothing at all had happened.

What caused Kitty to hide out behind the couch? Remember, she had been there since before I arrived home from work. What caused her to get spooked and go behind the couch? What made her get into her defensive stealth mode? What did she see in the back bedroom that had her taking steps backward? What did she see that I didn't see? And what was it that she stared and stared at? I don't know what she saw.

Whatever it was, it seems that it did not terrify or frighten her. I say this as Kitty's fur never stood up. I have seen cats get frightened and their hair does stand up and their tails will fluff up hugely. Not Kitty. But she was sure very cautious.

I didn't know what spooked Kitty. I didn't know what Kitty saw.

The next day, after reviewing this event over and over in my mind, I realized what Kitty had seen. I knew what it was that had spooked her yet did not terrify her. I knew what Kitty saw.

The day after that, Angel came to me, too, one last time.

Other Cats no longer in My Life - Schiz

I was reading the local weekly newspaper one day. That paper would print each week a photo of an animal up for adoption through the local shelter. His picture was there with his bio saying he had been there a very long time. Probably because he was shy when people wanted to look at him and he wasn't being very accommodating.

He reached out to me from that photo, and I drove over and got him. It was quite a time at the shelter, as he didn't want to go anywhere. They told me that he had finally got accustomed to life in the shelter.

While the paper work was being done, I was told he had been rescued from the local college, from a fraternity house where he had been abused. I asked the shelter aide what kind of abuse. She started to tell me, but then she shut up and I could not get her to tell me.

I took him home from the shelter and turned him loose in the house to find his way. I didn't see him for ten days. But I knew he was OK, as I saw the evidence in the litter box. And I knew he was OK when I didn't hear screeching from Kitty.

On the tenth day, I walked into a room he was in and he ran away.

On day fifteen, I was sitting at the table when I heard kitty feet coming down the steps from upstairs. He came around the corner and saw me and jumped up on the table. There we were, our faces at the same level, and he looked right at me. I raised a hand to pet him and he reared back and raised a paw to me. I remembered the aide at the shelter telling me that he had been abused. I could only imaging how badly.

But that day was a breakthrough day and the start of a great relationship. As time went on, his trust grew, and within a year, I was able to pet him without him drawing back in fear. The biggest plus however was that Kitty immediately was taken with him. That itself was a huge blessing.

A really remarkable thing about Schiz was that he was also a protector and bodyguard to the other cats. Whenever one of the guys would do something wrong, I would rant and rave and stomp my feet in such a way that the offender would know they had done something to displease me. One day, I was carrying on like this toward one of them when all of a sudden, I had ten claws and a mouth on my leg. It was Schiz.

After a few more occurrences like this, I came to realize that he didn't like me carrying on like that toward his roomies. The last time when I went off carrying on like I did, I stopped and looked behind me. There he was, crouching low and making his way toward me.

I quit using those antics after that. This put him at ease, and I never got surprised with ten claws and a mouth on my leg again. I know that all that abuse he had endured left an impression on him, and he must have thought I was being abusive toward the others when he came after me like he did.

He would always peer out the kitchen window when I got home. He would watch me for as long as I was outside, but when I opened the door and came inside, he wasn't there. But he would always be there watching out the window whenever I got home.

He always made me wonder when he would jump in bed with me and curl up where I could reach him. He would stay about twenty minutes as I read a book, then he would go on patrol. I never figured out what that was all about, but after I and the others was all settled in, he would take off for the basement and I would hear him down there roaming around, meowing. Then he would come back up and do the same going room to room in the house. Then he would get back in bed. Thus, I called it his "patrol."

And our time together was good and rewarding all the way up until cancer took him from me.

Schiz was a good cat and a good companion as long as I had him. But the manner of his passing was extraordinary.

One night after work, I was doing my self-imposed torture on my treadmill. I had the radio on to help alleviate the boredom, and Schiz had joined me by the treadmill and had curled up in one of the armchairs.

After a few minutes into my exercise, I heard the most terrible sound I had ever heard from a cat. It was a combination screech and howl and it came from Schiz. I rushed over to him in an instant. Schiz was lying on the cushion unresponsive and not breathing. I could see no sign of life in him. I was stricken. What happened?

Anyone who has ever lost a pet and held their dead animal knows what that feels like. The feel of holding their animal after the breath of life has left, just a limp object that once was a beloved pet.

Schiz was just like that. I sat with him for minutes. I was stunned. I had lost cats before but I had always known it was coming. I sat with him for about four minutes. I am being honest here because I know it was at least three minutes and it could have been as many as five minutes.

Then Schiz moved! He moved! He was still on the chair cushion and I was seated on the floor so my head was down next to him. And he moved; I felt him move. I sat up and he was looking at me like nothing had happened. I was astounded. I was all over him, petting him, hugging him, and talking to him until he became bored, jumped down, and went upstairs to check the food dish.

I was elated that Schiz was OK. I had thought he was dead. In my mind, he was dead. I went about my business that night and kept an eye on Schiz and he seemed to be fine.

The next day, I had misgivings about what happened and took Schiz to see Dr. Jackson. I explained what had happened. Dr. Jackson picked Schiz up and felt around beneath him like vets do when they are examining an animal. Then he told me, sadly, that Schiz had liver and pancreas cancer and there was nothing that could be done. When I asked Dr. Jackson how long he had, he said Schiz might live another ten days. He also informed me that there would be no pain in his passing. What a blessing! I wouldn't have to have him put down; I would have more time with my buddy.

But cancer? Where did cancer come from? I asked my vet. He reminded me of what I had completely forgotten that Schiz had been in about a year before and he had surgery to remove several lumps from his side. I remembered. I had completely forgotten that incident. The reason is that Schiz was the second cat I had that had lumps like that and had them removed. The first cat was Baby and he went on to live to be nineteen after Dr. Jackson removed his lumps. So when Schiz had his lumps removed, I did not give it another thought, as I was sure they were gone for good.

I took Schiz home. It was so hard to believe that he was going to die! He seemed fine. There was no change in his habits. Ten days came and went and Schiz was still fine, still the same old Schiz. On the eleventh day, a Sunday, I went out in the morning and came back. There was Schiz as usual looking at me out of the kitchen window. Inside, he was in the kitchen along with the other cats.

I went in the back room and I heard it again. I heard that same heart-rending wail sound I had heard twelve days before when I was on the treadmill. The sound was followed by the sound of claws scratching on the floor. I ran into the kitchen and Schiz was lying on his side. This time Schiz did not come back after four minutes. This time, I knew he wouldn't.

It wasn't until weeks later after I had been reviewing these events that I began to realize something special had happened with Schiz. I remembered when he had cried out when I was on my treadmill. I was convinced then that he had died. I had held him in my arms and he felt dead. He wasn't breathing. But I had overlooked this in the moment when he suddenly looked up at me. I had overlooked this because Dr. Jackson had told me I had ten more days with him. I was happy because I took a bunch of photos of him during those last ten days and I was able to psyche myself up for his passing.

Small Miracles

Did You See the Hand of God in Any of This?

When your read about each of my cats individually, did you see anything remarkable about certain incidents with them? Perhaps you did not see God in these accounts, but surely, you saw a remarkable string of coincidences. Maybe, you saw the hand of Mother Nature or maybe it was the Earth Mother or Tinkerbell.

Never fear, for I will relate the miracles that I saw and as I interpreted them. Keep in mind, I didn't see them at the time. It was not until after Pierre and Scaredy had returned after thirty-one days in the wilderness that I saw their return as a miracle. A *small miracle*. It was after that when I began reflecting on other odd happenings, happenings which I came to later see as *small miracles*. Here's my *small miracle* recap cat by cat. What do you think?

Pierre's Miracles

How and why did Pierre just wander into my life? What made him hang around after he showed up, and then take up residence in my garage? He was well fed and in good shape when he first showed up at my house. He was not a typical hungry stray, and his behavior after he got here was not that of a stray cat. Remember that I wrote that Pierre came and went for a while at first before he decided to stay around permanently.

I consider Pierre's arrival and his staying around afterward a *small miracle*. Yes, I know that stray cats will hang around anywhere where they can get a meal and shelter. But until Pierre arrived, I had many stray cats hanging around. The previous winter, I had noticed many cat tracks in the snow around my garage, and tracks going into the garage through the small cat door opening in the side. But I didn't have an outdoor cat at the time so none of the tracks were my cats. Also, I had got tired of putting uneaten cat food down the disposal and decided rather than waste it, I would put it out for whichever cats were hanging around. It worked; the food was eaten and didn't get wasted down the disposal. So for almost a year before Pierre showed up, I had plenty of stray cats coming around for a meal, but none stayed.

Next in terms of how I feel about Pierre and how we have bonded, I consider his presence here a *small miracle*. Why he stayed, I don't know. What drew him to hang around while none of the others stayed I can't begin to understand.

Later, Pierre and Scaredy were locked up for thirty days without food and water, and yet, they survived. The story of the both of them prompted two articles in my local *News Sun* newspaper.

Many said afterward that their being found was a miracle. In my interview with the *News Sun*, I said no, their being found was not the miracle. I said that the real miracle was whatever had kept two grown cats alive for thirty days in five-degree weather. Believe it or not, most responded by saying it must have been mice. Yes, mice. Mice are well known for roaming around in five-degree weather. And a whole lot of mice must have roamed around in that garage. Enough mice to keep two grown cats fed for thirty days. And some of the mice must have been packing a six-pack of unfrozen vitamin enriched spring water. And the tooth fairy will be stopping by tonight to settle up with me for all the teeth I no longer have.

I consider the survival of Pierre and Scaredy in extremely inclement weather for thirty days a *small miracle*.

I have to include one other thing about Pierre. A very strange occurrence, a *Twilight Zone* kind of thing. Not a small miracle as is the topic here but nevertheless something that is equally mysterious.

In the first few years with me, he would frequently jump up on my lap when I was sitting in the garage. I would pet him, talk to him, and comb his fur with a flea comb. Because of the strange way he had arrived at my place, I use to always ask him, "Who are you? Where did you come from?"

Those were tongue-in-cheek questions because I was then and still am, intensely curious about his existence before he showed up at my house.

One day, he was on my lap and I was combing him, and I asked him those questions. Only this time, I got an answer. In my head, as clear as if someone was standing next to me, I heard a reply. The answer was one short sentence that was both prophetic and scary. I am not revealing what he said as it is not pertinent to anything in this account. And I don't consider it a small miracle, either.

But it did give me a great deal to think about for the next few weeks and much material for many engaging philosophical conversations with myself. After several weeks, I no longer gave it any mind.

The Bible is clear about things like this. Voices in your head or from the "great beyond" are not to be trifled with. Because when all is said and done, you really don't know whom it was that was talking to you.

Scaredy's Miracles

As for Scaredy, how is it that she ended up in my life and in my garage? Just like Pierre, where did she come from and why did she stay? She was very feral and remains so, but to a much lesser degree, to this day. She does not like humans.

You could easily say she showed up and stayed because of the food scraps I was putting out. There is no miracle in that. Other critters often showed up for the handouts, so Scaredy being there was nothing unusual.

The miracle with Scaredy is for me. It is a miracle that goes on daily that happens to me. The *small miracle* is that I have been blessed enough to be able to provide for her. She is a true hobo that she gets so much from me and I get nothing in return. No rubbing against my leg, no purring when I pet her because she won't let me pet her, no snuggling in bed with me because I can't get her to come in the house. No, she takes and takes, and all I get is scolded if I'm late with the food.

When I noticed her hanging around, I began to put food out just for her. Then I began putting water out for her. On some days, other cats, raccoon, possum, and skunks come to my garage diner and share her food and water. She is still here after all this time.

I shared with you how I had got Scaredy a heater for in the cold weather and a water fountain for fresh water. I did this despite my frustration that she wouldn't come in the house where she would have had all the comforts of home, so to speak.

So I have this stray cat with her own heated apartment complete with running water. Pretty good for a stray. Pretty extravagant on my part too. Kind of eccentric, don't you think? (It's OK if you say yes.) Nothing miraculous in that except that I have been blessed to be able to provide all that for Scaredy, the stray cat that won't let me touch her and won't come in the house.

I say that the *small miracle* is that I am able to do this for Scaredy. Without getting into detail, I have been able to do this coming from a low-pay job and into fixed income retirement. I'm not complaining, mind you, only saying that despite this, I still am able to divert a small amount of my blessings for good old Scaredy the stray. And she still won't let me get near her.

Schiz's Miracles

Thinking about what you read about Schiz tell me how Schiz died in front of me and came back so that I was able to have two more weeks with him. The obvious is that **Schiz** wasn't dead; he was faking it just to shake me up or that he wasn't dead, he was just unconscious.

I am definitely not saying or even implying Schiz experienced any kind of resurrection in the biblical sense either. No way. Yet without CPR or medical electroshock or any medical action, he did come back after minutes of complete apparent lifelessness.

At the time when all that happened, I did not recognize what had happened. I have pondered this often. Schiz was gone but then he opened his eyes and seemed OK that night. Not realizing the significance of what had just happened, I left and went out to eat! It was not until many weeks after he was gone that it dawned on me that something special had happened that night.

Coincidence? The phase of the moon? All I know is I got to have him for eleven more days. To me, it was a *small miracle*.

Sweetie's Miracles

I told you how I ended up adopting Sweetie. But what about Sweetie's four siblings? I found homes for them all. Yet where did those four people come from who adopted them? They were four people who just happened to be looking to get a kitten and just happened to come into my life for only a moment. Just long enough to be able to take one of Scaredy's kittens from her very last litter at just the time I most needed to find homes for them? Today, I can't even tell you who three of those four people were. Was that coincidence?

No, I would not have taken the kittens to a shelter, but I would have kept them and continued to try to find a home for them. That would have put a real strain on resources already stretched.

To me, the arrival of those four people was a *small miracle*.

Kitty's Miracles

Thinking back on what you read about the day Kitty found me, how did I come to be by a particular bush at just the time when Kitty and her brother were hiding beneath it? I was on the roof of a ten-story building and I needed a hose that was on the ground by some of the landscaping. From the roof, I went down and got that hose.

And got Kitty. Five minutes, just five minutes in the passage of time, either way and things could have been a lot different.

As stated earlier, Kitty is very antisocial. One thing that I would pray from time to time was that Kitty would get along with Honey Bunny and Oscar, somehow, someway, before she passed away. I always thought Kitty was just Kitty, and at her age what could change her outlook toward Honey Bunny and Oscar? Well, this prayer was answered and was answered in a most peculiar way. Kitty had a stroke.

When I say "stroke," that is my diagnosis. I did not take Kitty to the doctor. I just based my conclusion on what I have read about strokes in humans and in cats. And cats are susceptible to strokes, especially as they get older.

One day, I woke up and Kitty was not Kitty. I thought that maybe she would die. She didn't do her usual actions, didn't go to her usual comfort places to nap and was very different, especially around me. In all other ways, she seemed healthy. After several days, she seemed to be coming out of it and her old peculiarities were slowly retuning. After about five days, most of her old ways were back, and she was back in bed with me in her usual spot, eating in her usual ways, and roaming the house in her usual ways.

Only three things were different and are different now. One, she gets along better with Honey Bunny. No, they're not cuddling buddies, but now when Honey Bunny comes near her Kitty no longer hisses, spits, or does her paw and claw waving. Kitty tolerates her and will now stay in the same room with her as long as Honey Bunny doesn't get too close. They even share one of the heater registers in winter and the sunlight inside the back door in summer. She only gets aggressive with Honey Bunny if Honey Bunny tries to cut in on Kitty when Kitty is on my lap or next to me on the bed.

The second change for Kitty is that she tolerates Oscar. Same conditions as with Honey Bunny.

The third change is that she will now occasionally just sit and stare. What she stares at or what is going on in her mind, I have no idea. But she does that, and I let her alone. The other cats let her alone as she sits and stares. But other than those three changes, Kitty seems to be the same Kitty as she was before her "stroke."

Was my prayer for Kitty to get along with Honey Bunny answered? To me, it was, and it was a *small miracle*. Or did Kitty just experience a "medical coincidence?"

I have mentioned that Kitty is showing signs of her age. She is now past her eighteenth year and more than half way toward nineteen, and the signs of her age are much more obvious.

Myself, I have been bracing for a feline funeral more than ever. Just bracing, mind you, just getting myself psyched up for the inevitable. I am leaving it to God as to when Kitty will leave me, and for all I know she'll be around for a few more years. Part of getting myself psyched up for when Kitty does leave me is gearing up for my grief that I know will follow her passing. She has been so close to me since I first brought her home. She has been in the bed with me since then, and for the past ten years since Schiz passed has been right next to me. Going to sleep at night, there's Kitty. Waking up, there's Kitty. Taking a nap, there's Kitty. Reading or watching a DVD, there's Kitty. So, I have been considering how I'm going to deal with the day when she is no longer there by me.

That day arrived some weeks ago. I woke up and she was not there. I figured the worse and went looking for her. I found her happily snoozing away in the kitchen in front of the dishwasher. And there she has been to this day.

Kitty has obviously undergone another personality change. She no longer gets in bed with me. She gets along well with all of her room mates. Even her dreaded Oscar and Honey Bunny. She gathers around the communal dish on the floor and eats along with her roomies, taking her turn when opportunity presents. She no longer gets on my lap when I'm reading or watching a DVD. She no longer will go to sleep in her basket on my desk when I'm on the computer. And most surprising she doesn't settle down in front of a heater outlet when the furnace comes on as she has always loved to do. She just has this spot by the dishwasher.

On the bright side she still has a very good appetite. Very good. She still knows where the food and the litter box are at, and hasn't confused the two. She has taken to drinking out of the toilet for the first time ever. She still craves affection and if I put her in my lap she climbs up and drapes herself across my chest and lets me pet her for hours. But she won't snooze. She still enjoys her backyard outings. And I can't bring her up to be with me when I'm on the computer. She sits directly in front of me on the desk and won't move.

So why do I bring all this up in the *Small Miracles* section? I believe I'm experiencing a *small miracle*, but this small miracle is for me. You see, in the past few weeks I'm getting used to Kitty not being in bed with me going to sleep or waking up. I'm getting used to Kitty not snoozing in my lap while I'm reading. I'm getting used to Kitty not being on my desk snoozing away next to me while I'm on the computer.

And while getting used to not having Kitty close to me I'm also a little amused at getting to know this new Kitty, this Kitty that actually likes her roommates and interacts with them.

Yes, I'm experiencing a *small miracle*.

Oscar's Miracles

I wrote about how I got Oscar, after he showed up where I worked but never left. I often think about how was it that Oscar never left that shop after wandering inside nor did he leave after several days—days when the big bay doors were wide open.

Most trapped animals would have run to daylight when trapped. Not Oscar. And how did he just happen to wander in to the company where I worked? It was summertime and every business in that complex had their bay doors open. He could have gone into any one of them. Oscar being there and not leaving to me was another *small miracle*. What was it to you, an accident?

Think about Oscar's trip to the doctor. Recall that I had finished cleaning the litter box in the basement and was ready to leave. For some reason I didn't. I stayed to change the deodorizer in the air filter. Remember how I saw Oscar in the litter box? That in itself was very, very unusual because Oscar never would use the litter box if I was near and he still won't to this day. Yet on that day there he was in the box and in position. If he had not tried to use the litter box in that exact window of time, I wouldn't have noticed his condition until later, possibly much later. Possibly even too late.

But he decided to go pee right then when I was there and I noticed his lack of success. Which enabled me to get him to the doctor in record time. A couple of amazing coincidences, huh?

I think that for both Oscar and me, it was a *small miracle*.

Honey Bunny's Miracles

Look at the circumstances how Honey Bunny came in to my life. I didn't even want her! And Honey Bunny is not what anyone would consider a cute cat. In an animal shelter, she would have been passed up over and over.

How did Honey Bunny heal so many times from so many serious health issues?

Honey Bunny experienced something very severe when she had her spinal stroke. I kept her confined in my bathroom for five weeks and she never once complained. She never once tried to get out. She sat there in her nest of piled up drop cloths for *five* weeks and never complained. How many animals would have done that? When I took her to the doctor five weeks later, she was walking again! Not a normal walk, but she was mobile. Was there not a *small miracle* with this?

Ah, you say, *but you said that on a latter visit to the emergency clinic you saw on X-rays where Honey Bunny had two vertebrae fused together?* You will also say, *you said that you figured that must have been Honey Bunny's problem back when she had her spinal stroke.* Based upon that, you would conclude that Honey Bunny had no miracle cure while she was penned up in my bathroom for five weeks.

Have you ever known anyone who has had back problems and they had discs that had deteriorated? I have. In certain back conditions, a medical procedure is performed to fuse the patient's vertebrae together as a treatment. Doctors do this medically, as with Tiger Woods. There were no doctors in my bathroom while Honey Bunny was restrained there for five weeks. No human doctors.

Today, Honey Bunny continues to persevere. She walks funny, and she has diminished lung capacity. She coughs from time to time, sometimes for up to a minute. I have to clean her almost daily. I worry endlessly about her.

Honey Honey's Miracles

I got Honey Honey because I had asked my friend Susan for a kitten. Susan picked Honey Honey out of a batch of kittens. What made her pick Honey Honey? Coincidence?

Honey Honey fell out of my upstairs window and was gone for five days and returned. I'm not saying that was a miracle, but I am saying I was certainly blessed when she did return.

Another thing about Honey Honey that is not in itself miraculous but surely contains a life lesson for us. I previously related how Honey Honey has no teeth. It's marvelous that she doesn't realize that she has no teeth. Therefore she is able to eat whatever food I put out at feeding time. I imagine she grinds her food with her gums. Or she swallows whole. I do know that she does not have any digestive issues.

Likewise with no teeth she is unable to groom herself and despite my best efforts with brush and scissors her coat is full of tangles. Some of which get quite large. And I can't cut them off until they grow out enough for me to be able to get the scissors beneath them to cut them off. So she goes through life with these big lumpy tangles all over her body.

Honey Honey is not aware that she is supposed to have teeth. Likewise Honey Honey is not aware that her fur is supposed to be smooth, tangle free, and silky. For Honey Honey having these big tangles on her is normal. Honey Honey accepts life as it was given to her and makes the best of each day.

I'm sure there is a lesson here for deep thinkers and moralists.

Honey Honey has been an exceptional pet and has been healthy during her whole time with me. Is that a coincidence? Good luck? Alignment of the stars? I think that since I have had no medical problems with her that in itself is a *small miracle*.

All the Cats

When Schiz died, I was sad on two fronts. One was that he had died. The other was I was positive Kitty was going to go any day afterward. The reason? I had only had one cat up to this time that got to a double-digit age. None of my cats, other than Baby who was about nineteen when he left me, had ever made it to ten years old. Including Schiz. So I was sure Kitty was next.

As this goes to press, six of the seven cats you read about are over ten years of age. I find this remarkable. I find this wonderful. I attribute this to *small miracles*.

Man, Animals and God

When some terrible atrocity is committed on people, especially on children, here they come, the atheists. Ready to point out that if there was a God why would He allow such a terrible thing to happen to these people.

Likewise, when some atrocity is committed on an animal or animals, the atheists are there to say that if there were a God why would He let that happen to a poor defenseless animal?

Stop!

Man, not God, brings on those atrocities to humans and animals. Man who can make choices does them. God gave mankind that ability to make choices. Man has freewill. When you hear about the terrible acts on humans or animals, know that it is a man who did it and it happened because a man made the choice to do it. God did not "allow" it any more than he allows any of the Ten Commandments to be broken.

Do not worry about the animals; they are in God's hands, as you are, if you truly believe.

Do you ever think about the differences between man and animals? Man has freewill and animals don't. Man can act on logic and intelligence and animals act on instinct and smell.

The words of the Bible and the lessons to be learned therein are all about the salvation of man, about his eternal soul, not about animals, their well-being, or their afterlife.

Man, Cats, Other Animals and Heaven

Did people even have pets during biblical times? We know they had animals, all kinds of animals. Animals were their currency, their heavy labor, their sustenance and their very existence. But did they have special animals that got special treatment, even loved? Animals not destined for the dinner table? Pets? I'm sure they did. It's human nature.

And it is so today. We humans become very attached to our pets. We suffer along with them when they suffer. When they are pleased, we are pleased. When they pass on, we grieve.

Like many, after losing a few of my cats, my beloved companions, I found myself wondering the age-old question—do animals have souls?

I believe animals have a spirit. The Bible tells us that both man (Genesis 2:7) and animals (Genesis 1:30) have the breath of life. It is the spirit that animates them, the spirit of life. But do they have a soul? No, I don't believe animals have a soul in the sense that humans have a soul or in any sense. I don't believe cats or any other animal will have to ever account for their actions to their Creator. By their very nature, animals are sinless and thus have no need of a soul or even a conscience. They do what they have been "programmed" to do. That is, they do what they were *created* to do by the Creator.

> Jesus said that not a sparrow falls to earth
> that the Father does not know about it.
> ***(Mat 10:29)***

When Jesus said that our Father knows when every sparrow falls most assuredly, He knows when every cat passes away.

> "And the dust returns to the earth as it once was,
> and the spirit returns to God who gave it."
> ***(Ecc 12:7)***

So we see that God knows what is going on here on earth, but why would Jesus use a sparrow falling to earth to show it? Why didn't he use a baby as the example? Surely, people could relate more closely to a sweet little baby when considering the words of Jesus. So why use a sparrow?

I believe there is a message in the message. God is not merely tracking each sparrow. He knows about each sparrow because each is part of His creation and there is something more for that sparrow than just putting in a brief appearance on Earth.

I believe the same for cats and other animals. And isn't it for all the fallen sparrows to become a part of God's kingdom in heaven?

If God knows of each teeny-tiny sparrow, what more could there be? Since He knows about each sparrow, surely He knows about you. Big you, small sparrow. Big miracles, small miracles.

Biblical prophecy states that in the millennial kingdom the lion and the lamb will lie down together, and a child shall lead them (Isaiah 65:25).

This is also another message in a message. If there is a lion and a lamb in the millennial kingdom, is it not safe to assume that there will also be cats? Hmm. As far as heaven we don't know whether our pets will be there. We don't even know if there will be any animals. But we trust in God, don't we?

> "I know that all God does lasts forever;
> there is no adding to it or taking from it"
> **(Ecc 3:16.)**

Me, My Cats, and God

I still seek the path to God and salvation or I should say I seek to remain on the path. It is a path on which it is easy to take a wrong turn. I believe in God and I believe in miracles. Read on and you will see.

When you were reading this, whether reading this one year or fifty years after it was written, be comforted that you were reading about seven living cats, Kitty, Oscar, Honey Bunny, Honey Honey, Pierre, Scaredy, and Sweetie. I wanted very much to finish this while they were all alive and healthy and I have succeeded. These cats are alive and in my life now at this moment.

I wanted you to know about my cats. In knowing about my cats, I wanted you to know God and to know He is real. I hope I have written well enough for you to see why they are so special to me and how through them I got closer to God. Most of all, I also hope that this helps you to get closer to God.

I see God in my cats when they breathe. I hear them purr, and in their purr, I hear God. I feel close to God when I am close to my cats. Through these *small miracles* related here that God has granted my cats, He has reached me.

Cats love to bask in the sunlight. They are so still and move as needed as the sun makes its way across the sky and that spot of light makes its way across the floor. There they are, so still, basking away, eyes not quite closed and not quite asleep. Maybe they know something I don't know. Hmm.

> Be still, and know that I am God.
> Psalm 46:10

Remember that I wrote that I tried to join the army three times? And three times, there was a miscue of some kind that left me still a civilian. Three times, I tried to join the army at a time when the army was desperate to sign anyone who could chew gum and walk at the same time. There was a war on the horizon and there were quotas to be filled. Where would I be today if I had succeeded at one of those three attempts? Where would I be today if I had tried a fourth time to join the Army and been successful?

Was it the sun god who interfered with my three attempts to enlist in the army? Were the stars not aligned just right? Or could it have been something more, something divine? I used to wonder about that. But not anymore.

I often consider how much richer my bank account would be if it wasn't for all the cats I have and have had. Then I consider how much richer I have become because I have had these cats.

For example, my first life-enriching event out of many that I had as a result of having cats was about my feelings toward dogs. I hated dogs. As a child, I would go out of my way to hurt a dog. That was mostly because dogs did not like me. My parents often told me of my getting savaged by a dog when I was very small. I don't remember that event, but I do remember several other run-ins with dogs, some of which ended with me getting medical attention. People's dogs that had never ever bitten anyone else would bite me. Go figure.

I changed that attitude about dogs soon after I had my first two cats, and since then, I have not had any trouble with dogs. I have friends and neighbors with dogs and I like them all and get along with them just fine. They're my special dog buddies.

I pray for my cats. And I am sad doing it, knowing how many other cats are in need all over our country and the world and all the humans also in need and in need of prayer. And I know there are many.

I also pray that those who are adrift could find their own cats or dogs or goldfish. I pray that they could find whatever they need to anchor them to a world other than this world, to anchor them to this life and then to life eternal. It can be done.

In the preface, I expressed my wish that you would see the hand of God in these events. Did I succeed? I am sure that those who were believers before reading this will still be believers. Possibly, even strengthened by this account. I am equally sure that those die-hard nonbelievers haven't changed their beliefs either, self-assured that everything I related here was just my good luck or coincidence. For those persons, I can only hope that you enjoyed reading about my cats and hope that in the future you will have a change of heart. Before it is too late.

I can tell you that what you read about here it is not good luck or coincidence as I have been buying lottery tickets as long as I have had my cats, and there has been no good luck or coincidences with that.

But what about those people who are in the middle? Those unsure people, those who are wavering, those who need an event or message to nudge them in the right direction, what about them? Are you one of them? Did the *small miracles* here nudge you? Did reading this cause you to reevaluate your outlook or to reexamine your beliefs? Can you not see that a belief in God is not just about the collection plate on Sunday or an itinerary of dos and don'ts for your life?

Man, Cats, Love and God

Love. Other languages have different words that all mean love in love's various forms. We as humans love our mother.

We also love ice cream. But we love our cats more than ice cream. And we really love a good baseball game. But the word love for our children is oh so special. In English, we derive the intensity of the love from the context in which it is used.

So where does all this love that we have come from? Isn't love itself more intense than just a feeling? We have feelings that can get hurt and we have feelings when we hear about some tragedy. We have a feeling for someone we just met. The feeling may grow stronger over time. Then the feeling grows so strong it becomes love.

Love for one's mate or children is surely the most intense form of feelings or love that we have. Where then do humans get the capability to have feelings or to have love? We know animals display very strong protective traits for their offspring and will even die protecting them from danger. But is that love? Is that even a feeling? It isn't and we call it instinct. The same mother who will fight to the death to protect her cub will chase it from the den when the time comes. Once again, instinct.

So where did humans get their love? Evolution? Why, that's the catchall, end-all for many scientists who work in the various fields of biology from one-cell creatures all the way to humans.

If evolution is such great concept where are the six legged creatures? Where are the two-headed creatures? Why is it that most all higher forms of life have a body, four limbs or appendages, one head, two eyes, one mouth, two lungs, etc., etc., etc. Not a lot of variation like one would expect from random evolution. In fact, even in fossil records, there are no such variations.

So then, if mankind evolved from slime and worked its way up the evolutionary ladder to the apes, and then *shazam*, up popped Homo sapiens, where then did we pick up the ability to have feelings and to love?

If you read books on love and all its aspects, you will find no reference to evolution. If you read books on evolution, you will find no reference to love.

We are created beings, created by our creator, God. When we were created, we were given freewill. Don't you think maybe we also were given the ability to love about then too? It makes sense to me. What do we read about in the Bible going back to earliest times? Love. The Old Testament is packed full of love. Good love, bad love, physical love, erotic love, parental love, sibling love, love of the land, and love of the creator God.

And it is full of God's love for us. We know God made us in his image, so don't you think he passed on that ability to love to us? So we could give and receive love?

And if all that love in the Old Testament wasn't enough then along comes the New Testament and we are drenched with a new love.

"For God so loved the world that he gave his only begotten son and who so ever believes in him shall not perish but have eternal life." **John 3:16**

You really need to understand the full ramifications of this verse.

Can you love an animal that just wandered in to your life? Can you adopt an animal from a life of cages in a shelter? Can you go all out to save that animal from sickness or injury? And can you grieve mightily for the loss of your animal? That is love. If you can say yes to any of those questions how can you not believe that there is a God and how can you not believe in God?

If you can do any or all that it should be easy to realize that God feels the same way about you. He does love you, and He can go all out to save you. Yes, He can save you from sickness and injury, but mostly He can save you from yourself. He does and He will.

You did not just wander into His life like how Pierre wandered into my garage one night. He created you and He gave you your life. And through His son, Jesus Christ, he can give you eternal life.

Do not make the mistake of thinking you are assured a place in heaven because you are kind to animals or because you volunteer at the nursing home or donate to the Red Cross.

*He saved us - not by works of righteousness that we had done, but according to his MERCY.
Titus 3 verse 5*

This is the same mistake self-righteous people make—sure that they will get their place in heaven because they are *good people*. How many people do you know who tell you that they will be in heaven "*because I am a good person?*" That is about as meaningful as those who tell you they don't believe in God but they are "spiritual."

If a person thinks they are a Christian and will get to heaven only because they are a "good person," then they are not truly a Christian and do not understand the Crucifixion.

There is only one way to heaven and that is through the Lord Jesus Christ, not through all the good deeds in the world.

> *I am the way, the truth, and the life: no*
> *man cometh unto the Father, but by me.*
> John 18:8

If all it takes to get to heaven is to be good then there was no need for Jesus to ever be born in Bethlehem and then die on the cross for your sins. But He did and He did it out of love.

You Decide

Until I got this collection of cats, I had been a two-cats-at-a-time person, especially with my kind of work and being gone long hours, sometimes days. My thinking was with two cats, they would at least have some companionship during those periods of my absence.

Logic dictates that if you have two cats, there will be differences between the two. Cats are cats, aren't they? It wasn't until I got these seven cats living all together that I realized just how different cats are from each other. Just like seven people.

The seven cats have seven separate personalities and separate likes and dislikes. This goes for food, sleeping spots, the amount of attention they like, and their voices. They are like all cats, but they are seven separate little personalities unto themselves. Amazing.

When I move about my home and weave in and out of six cats lying about underfoot, I look at them and I see six miracles. When I go outside, I see a seventh miracle living in my garage.

Sometimes, though, when I am going about the house being thankful for my blessings, I pause to think, "What if I'm not the one that's blessed? What if it's these seven cats that are blessed, and I am just the instrument of that blessing?"

Either way, it is still the hand of God.

Please think about all I have related here. What are the odds on so many coincidences, so much luck?

Believe.

Extra - You've Lost Your Cat - Now What?

You have lost your cat.

The words here are not meant to console you or give you spiritual or philosophical wisdom that will soothe your soul and mend those feelings you are experiencing over the loss of your friend, your cat.

Though I truly wish they could.

I have experienced those feelings more than once and I would have given anything for something to grasp onto that would make the pain go away. No, these words are for after you have come to terms with your loss. I truly hope that you find in here advice that helps you decide what to do now.

Your loss happened from the following:

- Death due to natural or accidental causes.
- It went missing and was never found.
- Or some other obscure way.

You've lost your cat.
Your buddy.
Your best friend.
Your companion.
Your gift from God.

Now, you have to decide what you are going to do.

Three common choices:

Number 1. "I'm never going to have another cat. I just can't go through this pain again."

Number 2. "I'm going to find another cat just like Fluffy."

Number 3. "I'm going to get a cat or kitten and start a new relationship with another cat that I can love."

Before I talk about these three choices, I want to tell you about an experience I had years before this writing.

I was driving to a friend's house one day and lying on the centerline in the road was a cat. I had seen many cats and other critters lying on the road after having been hit by a car, who hasn't? What was different about this one was that it was not squished.

After driving past, I got to thinking, "What if the cat wasn't dead? What if it was only unconscious?" I returned to where the cat was and upon picking it up, I could tell it was dead. But this was no stray cat. Its fur was clean and neat and it was very well fed. It had to be someone's pet. A nice cat like this surely had a home.

Trying to find out from the homes on each side of the road was fruitless; no one knew anything. No one saw anything. No one was saying anything. Just like on those cop shows where there are a hundred witnesses but no one saw anything.

I took that cat home and treated it as one of my own by burying it amongst my own.

I was positive this cat was someone's pet and that whoever they were they would be wondering where Fluffy was. The next day, I took out ads in the *Cleveland Plain Dealer* and the *Sun News* as finding a lost cat. I did not mention in the ad that the cat was deceased. I described the cat and the exact location where I found it. My thinking was that at least if I got a call, I would be able to let someone know why their cat never came home and that it got a decent burial.

I never got that call from that someone and this saddened me very much. I even went back a week later and drove all over that area to see if anyone had put up notices on telephone poles about a lost cat. Once again no luck. How sad.

However, I did get some phone calls in response to my ad. This too was a sad experience for me as I talked to about six people whose cats had got out and disappeared, or were outside cats and didn't come home. The people were very grief-stricken and would have given anything to get their cats back. There was only one person who called who was anywhere close to where I had found the cat, and he was two miles away. One person called from over fifty miles away!

The cat I found was not the one these people were looking for. But I took time to talk to these people and try to give them some comfort. Later, I committed some of my thoughts to paper in the hope they could help someone else at some future time.

Now back to choices 1, 2, and 3 and some things you should consider.

Choice 1. "I'm never going to have another cat again. I just can't go through this pain again."

This is probably a normal emotion that everyone goes through in those first few days after a loss or at the moment when you realize your lost cat is really lost. I know I have. But don't most people come around after a few days or a few weeks? I think so and people I have talked to confirm this. If you start out with choice 1, then odds are you will eventually move to choice 2 or 3.

But what if you don't? What if you remain adamant on choice 1? That is your choice, of course. And no one would blame you if you held this position.

OK, be that way, but consider this. You, as a person who was a loving cat owner, are now denying a home to some cat, somewhere. Some stray or some cat in some shelter. Think about it. You're sitting there alone in your grief while there is a cat out there somewhere without a home, without the kind of love and care that it can only get from being in a stable human home. From you.

Choice 2. "I'm going to find another cat just like Fluffy."

This is another understandable reaction to losing your cat. You want to get another cat as soon as possible and you want it to be just like your lost Fluffy. Look around at the shelters long enough and you will find a cat that looks enough like your lost Fluffy that it could be Fluffy's twin. You scoop it up and take it home with you.

Here are the facts. The cat you just brought home may look like Fluffy but it is not Fluffy and it won't become Fluffy. The person who does this may come to realize that and then come to resent the new cat because it isn't Fluffy. And when the resentment starts that will only lead to worse things that will happen.

Instead of getting a cat just like Fluffy, why not just get a cat and love it just like you loved Fluffy?

Choice 3. "I'm going to get a cat or kitten and start a new relationship with another cat that I can love."

This is another understandable reaction after losing your cat. And there is nothing wrong with this choice.

Here are some facts to consider when replacing a lost cat. These are only meant as things to consider and are in no way a condemnation of you if you choose to not consider these things. These items to consider could also be used if you are thinking of getting a second (or third) cat for your family. After all, the most important thing is to get another cat out of a shelter or off the streets and into a good home.

Picking out a cat. *Considerations before* **buying or adopting.**

Kittens—any cat lover loves kittens. Kittens *always* get adopted. Young children usually always will pick out a kitten when selecting a new pet. Adults love kittens. Just one thing to remember—for every kitten that goes home with someone, an adult cat does not go home.

My friend Susan used to pound this into me. Susan was a big proponent of spaying and neutering so that there wouldn't be such a supply of kittens.

So what to *consider* here is "do you really need a kitten?"

Look-a-likes—choosing a cat that looks just like the one you lost *may* be a disappointment. Your new cat can only look like your lost cat and it can never be like your lost cat. It will be its own cat and its relationship with you will develop as time goes by and will probably be just as rewarding a relationship as what you had with your lost cat. Don't expect a cat that looks like your lost cat to be like your lost cat. So *consider* if you really want to find a cat that is a look alike for your lost cat.

Potluck cats – You've decided to get another cat to replace the one you lost. You love cats and you're over the loss of your previous cat and are ready to move on.

Instead of going to the cat shelter(s) and going down the rows and picking out a real nice looking cat, *consider* this: don't go "cat shopping." Going up and down the rows is OK for buying a used car. Not necessarily for adopting a cat into your home.

Instead, call up your local no-kill shelter and ask for the cat that's been there the longest. Then, go to the shelter, get it, and take it home. Have them have it ready to go when you get there. When you get there, get it and go home.

Why? There are always a few cats that get passed by. They get passed by again and again. They just aren't quite as cute as the cat in the next cage. They just don't seem to be as receptive to having fingers stuck in their cage as the cat two cages over. They are just shy. And as such they get passed by once more, again and again. You, as a cat lover, need to be aware of this. The cute cats and the finger receptive cats always go home with someone.

If you go "cat shopping," you are most likely to go home with a cute, pretty, or adorable cat. People are people, and they tend to gravitate toward that which is attractive.

People, remember this. You are there to get a cat. You are not picking out a used car! Looks don't matter when it comes to cats. Cute, pretty, and adorable cats don't always make good pets. Keep that in mind.

You, as a cat lover looking to take home a cat, have a chance to do something really good here. Take home the cat that has been at the shelter the longest and start to explore what a great relationship you can have with your new "pot luck" kitty.

Maybe it isn't cute, maybe it could care less about your finger waving around in its face, but that doesn't mean it doesn't deserve a home, and it doesn't mean it won't be a great cat once it realizes that it has security, food, and shelter—it has a home. Think of all the joy you will have finding out what it does care about. Take it home and give it a free rein. As time goes by, who knows, maybe it will come around on that finger wagging.

Oh yes, the reason I said to just go there and get it is because we are all human, and if you start looking around or cat shopping and seeing all those cute cats, the finger cats, well, you don't want to do that. Take home the cat you called about.

Senior Cats—You've decided to get another cat to replace the one you lost. You love cats and you're over the loss of your previous cat and are ready to move on.

Instead of going to the cat shelter(s) and going down the rows and picking out a real nice looking cat, *consider* this: don't go cat shopping. Call up your local no-kill shelter and ask for the cat that they believe is the oldest in age. That's right. Then, go to the shelter, get it, and take it home. Have them have it ready to go when you get there, and when you get there, get it, and go home. Why? The seniors always get passed by. And they get passed by again and again and again. The reasons are obvious.

The senior cats almost always do not go home with someone. You, as a cat lover, looking to take home a cat has a chance to do something really, really, really special here. Take home the senior cat. It may have been at the shelter a long time. Yes, I know what you're thinking, "but it's old, it might die soon." True, but you really don't know when it will die or when any cat you take home will die. Then again, you don't know when you will die, either. It may live to twenty, who knows? But if it doesn't just think of the good you have done for yourself and for the senior cat for however many years you get blessed with to be together. Think seriously about taking home a senior.

After all of the foreclosures in the past years, thousands of people have moved out and abandoned their pets. Because of this, the shelters today are full of many fine cats (and other pets.) Because they are no-kill shelters, they have cats that aren't cute. They have old cats. Some even have handicapped cats. They have kittens. If you are looking for a cat or a kitten, it is a buyers' market.

My purpose for writing this topic is to have you consider *all* aspects when picking out a new cat. It is always best to have as many facts as possible so as to make the right decision. Remember, you are starting out again to begin a relationship that will last till death do you part.

Don't you wish you could find a human companion that easily?

About the Author

Woodrow "Woody" VanKirk was honorably discharged from the US Navy in 1969, and using the education he received from the Navy, obtained employment as a service tech in the up and coming wonderful world of computers. There was much traveling involved and some were overnight trips. Woody discovered that a cat was the perfect pet for this type of a job and got his first cat in 1970. Work in the wonderful world of computers ended in 1997 but the wonderful world of cats did not. Woody is now retired and lives alone with his seven cats.

CPSIA information can be obtained
at www.ICGtesting.com
Printed in the USA
BVHW02s2130270318
511745BV00017B/181/P